THE
INVISIBLE
LEADER

THE
INVISIBLE
LEADER

TRANSFORM Your Life, Work, *and* Organization
***with the* POWER *of* AUTHENTIC PURPOSE**

ZACH MERCURIO

Advantage.

Published by Advantage, Charleston, South Carolina.
Member of Advantage Media Group.

ADVANTAGE is a registered trademark, and the Advantage colophon is a trademark of Advantage Media Group, Inc.

Printed in the United States of America.

10 9 8 7 6

ISBN: 978-1-59932-851-5
LCCN: 2017945558

Cover & layout design by Melanie Cloth.

This publication is designed to provide accurate and authoritative information in regard to the subject matter covered. It is sold with the understanding that the publisher is not engaged in rendering legal, accounting, or other professional services. If legal advice or other expert assistance is required, the services of a competent professional person should be sought.

Advantage Media Group is proud to be a part of the Tree Neutral® program. Tree Neutral offsets the number of trees consumed in the production and printing of this book by taking proactive steps such as planting trees in direct proportion to the number of trees used to print books. To learn more about Tree Neutral, please visit **www.treeneutral.com.**

Advantage Media Group is a publisher of business, self-improvement, and professional development books. We help entrepreneurs, business leaders, and professionals share their Stories, Passion, and Knowledge to help others Learn & Grow. Do you have a manuscript or book idea that you would like us to consider for publishing? Please visit **advantagefamily.com** or call **1.866.775.1696.**

To my wife, Erin, and my son, Tapley, who are my ultimate purpose. To my parents, who never pressured me to be anything other than who I am. Thank you.

TABLE OF CONTENTS

DISCLAIMER

In an effort to weave my personal experience into parts of this book, I have tried to recreate events and conversations from my memories of them. In order to maintain anonymity in some instances I have changed or omitted the names of individuals, organizations, and places. I also may have changed some identifying characteristics and details of such individuals or organizations.

ACKNOWLEDGMENTS

My fascination with purpose was inspired by every "teacher" I've had in my life.

And so, thank you:

To all of my students, for sharing your lives and experiences with me—particularly to the students in my "Leading with Authentic Purpose" courses who implored me to write this book.

To my supervisors and mentors: Steve Grande, my supervisor in college, who taught me what authenticity is and Kerry Wenzler, a mentor and supervisor in graduate school who allowed me to experiment with training people with purpose.

To all my professors and academic mentors, specifically Dr. Carlos Aleman and Dr. Russ Korte who instilled a passion for research and curiosity.

To the leaders of the purpose and meaningful work movements and my personal inspirations: Aaron Hurst, Simon Sinek, Adam Grant, Dr. Bryan Dik, Brandon Peele, and Paul Ratoff, and the growing community of researchers and influencers who exist to help people thrive.

To all the anonymous people who have impacted me along the way and especially the ordinary people with extraordinary perspectives—especially a certain Washington, DC cab driver who helped point me toward my life's authentic purpose.

THE TRANSFORMATIVE POWER OF PURPOSE

The search for purpose and meaning is fundamentally human—the unifying trait of our species.

Our yearning for purpose begins (to many new parents' dismay) as soon as we learn language. As I write these words, my two-year-old has just learned the immense value of questioning to make sense of the world. It comes as no surprise that like countless other toddlers, he incessantly asks, "Why?"

These three letters represent, in my view, the most powerful question in human language—and the hardest to answer. When we ask *why* we seek a *reason*, a justification for the existence of whatever we're inquiring about. We seek a purpose. But the answer to *why* is perhaps more transformative than the question. When we ask *why* of ourselves or our organizations, the answer is our purpose. Purpose is our reason for existence, the answer to the question: Of what use are we to the world?

When stated clearly and enacted consistently, purpose has the power to unite, compel, engage, and transform our lives, our organizations, and the world.

THE NEED FOR PURPOSE

The need to share the ideas and research in this book came from listening intently to our future leaders in high schools and universities, organizational leaders, employees in diverse occupations, and researchers dedicating their life's work to better understanding human motivation and thriving.

And what I've heard is clear: People are longing for purpose more than ever in school, work, and life.

And I've also uncovered critical tensions. While human beings are wired for purpose (or *why),* our systems and institutions continue to be motivated by and obsessed with results (or *what).*

For instance:

- While researchers find that students perform better when they know the other-centered, larger purpose of a task, we still measure them by arbitrary grades and degrees.

- Even though we know that existential confusion is one of the leading causes of clinical anxiety and depression among college students, institutions increasingly tout high starting salaries and job placement statistics to lure and motivate students.

- While we know that people generally want to contribute to some greater good in society and have a natural desire for meaningful work, we still overwhelmingly measure them by quotas and targets, and we judge their worth with money alone.

- And even though we know from extensive worldwide research that people generally work for more than money and benefits, workplaces are in a race to offer the best salaries, the best benefits, and the most ping-pong tables and slides in their offices.

Such tensions might partly explain why the Gallup organization repeatedly finds just 13 percent of the world's workforce likes going to work, despite the rise of popular books and research on employee engagement, organizational culture, and motivation. Or why the upcoming millennial generation will hold more jobs over their lifetimes than previous generations. Or why depression and anxiety among college students in the job-placement era are increasing.

These tensions are precisely why this book exists: to help people tap into their own and others' natural desire for purpose and to change our systems, institutions, and lives to unleash the researched power of purpose.

ABOUT "THE INVISIBLE LEADER"

This book is personal for me.

My own story of being purposeless and a chance encounter with a purposeful cab driver, which I'll get to in a later chapter, led me to write these very words.

I saw the existential confusion and pressures to achieve and acquire "things" inflicted on college students when

I worked in higher education for nearly a decade, and I continue to see them now, teaching and conducting research as a PhD student at a large research university. In my work as a speaker and trainer for a wide variety of organizations, from nonprofits to Fortune 500 companies, I have found that meaningful work is not about high salaries and perks but in doing work that matters to the world.

This is most likely why the most successful people and organizations I've worked with don't focus obsessively on results such as profit but on justifying their reason for existence. When they do that, the results follow.

In fact, research shows that a compelling and other-centered authentic purpose—"The Invisible Leader"—may be the most powerful influencer of our behaviors, attitudes, and motivation in organizations, work, school, and life.

Anyone who sees himself or herself as a leader can benefit from this book, and my definition of "leader" here is broad. It includes CEOs and the executive directors of non-profits but also anyone leading a group project in a class, a work group, a volunteer effort, a family, a friendship, or a life (which is all of us).

Becoming more purposeful begins with changing our mindset and beliefs about our world. This book revolves around three core beliefs that form the foundations for its sections:

1. The belief that we and what we do matters

2. The belief in a bigger, other-centered purpose

3.   The belief in proving that purpose consistently

WHAT TO EXPECT

In Part I, I'll explore what authentic purpose is and the power of invisible leadership from a research and case study perspective. The next section will help you learn how to adopt a purposeful mindset and instill it within your life and organization. Finally, I'll explore how to deliver purpose on a daily basis.

While I present plenty of academic research as well as case studies and personal anecdotes that demonstrate the well-documented power of the invisible leader, this is not meant to be a theoretical book. The research is included to build a case and to provide a foundation for practical action. Most chapters include a mix of philosophy, psychology, anecdotes, and research, but I want to highlight for readers the "Practicing Purpose" exercises at the end of each chapter.

I know it can be tempting to skip such exercises. Some readers might see the whole idea of purpose as "fluffy," as one CEO told me. My answer to that take—one I have tried very consciously to address here—is that purpose is only fluffy when we don't strategize around it and actively pursue it.

The Practicing Purpose exercises at the end of each chapter provide a practical, concrete way to put purpose into action. The key to making this book useful is to engage in the process outlined in those exercises.

By awakening authentic purpose, we can build environments and systems that leverage our own and others' natural desire for meaning. We can use that desire to inspire, compel, and ultimately empower sustainable lives and organizations, and in the process, we can address some of the most pressing issues our society faces.

THE PATH TO PURPOSE

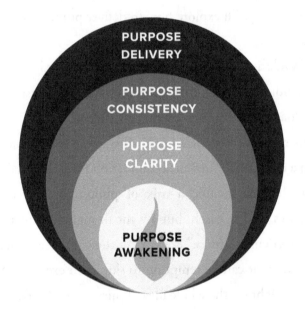

PART I

AUTHENTIC PURPOSE: THE INVISIBLE LEADER

CHAPTER 1

WHAT IS AUTHENTIC PURPOSE?

He who has a why to live can bear almost any how.

—*Friedrich Nietzsche*

Mary spent twenty-five years as a custodian, cleaning the bathrooms, rooms, and hallways of university dormitories. She diligently worked her way up to a supervisor position before retiring to spend more time with family and friends. Her retirement didn't last long. She returned to the entry-level custodian position she'd started more than twenty-five years ago—cleaning the same dormitories.

I had the pleasure of interviewing "Mary" for a pilot research project I conducted on how people find meaning in work. I asked her, "Why return to a job you've already spent decades in?" Her answer became one of my prime motivations for writing this book.

"I couldn't stand the thought of those students not having a parent figure away from home," I remember her saying.

This was how she saw herself, as a parent figure for college students. She told me that she talked to them about classes, worries, stress. They shared with her details of their lives in their hometowns. She counseled them as a kind of guardian while they lived away from their families.

Mary's purpose was bigger than she was—so powerful, in fact, it brought her back to do the job again.

Cleaning was *what* she did. Supporting and connecting with students was *why* she did it.

I spoke to Mary's supervisors. They never told her that she should serve as a critical support system for students. They offered no formal training or employee onboarding around the idea, no mentoring program or HR interventions on being a "parent figure." They didn't give her a bonus or a promotion for taking time to connect with students.

PRACTICING PURPOSE TIP

Identify barriers in your personal and organizational life to being purpose-led. Keep these in mind for the rest of the book.

She had awakened her authentic purpose, the real reason the job existed in the first place: to help people graduate from college.

This purpose—what I and others have called the "invisible leader"—was such a powerful psychological and motivational force that it *pulled* her out of retirement.

Hearing her story, I wondered what would happen if all custodians on campus were told from their first interviews that they existed to be supporters of students' lives. What if their training also emphasized this kind of service and they were supervised as if their jobs truly mattered in the world? What if they were instilled with the same sense of authentic purpose that Mary discovered on her own?

Thinking about the university's custodians led me to consider its students. I imagined how higher education might change if they, too, were guided by this kind of authentic purpose—if they were asked *why* before making decisions about *how* and *what*. What if students sought to awaken the purpose of their academics, extracurricular activities, majors, and potential careers? And what if the leaders in the companies, nonprofits, schools, and research laboratories where those students later went to work put a compelling purpose at the core of all they did? What if everyone—politicians, CEOs, salespeople—were led by a compelling purpose beyond self, one that seeks to better the lives of others?

Like Mary, most of us lead our lives without someone constantly telling us what to do or believe. Our motivation comes from something deeper and less obvious, something almost invisible. Authentic purpose is that invisible leader, and research finds that it's one of the most powerful and sustainable motivators of human beings.

Everything we do, every job we have, and every organization we work in has a world-changing reason for existence. When we focus on that reason, results follow.

But what is "authentic purpose?" How do we awaken it in our lives, work, schooling, and organizations? How do we create environments that foster the inherent human search for purpose?

This book will offer answers to these questions and provide practical and research-backed ways of putting authentic purpose—the invisible leader—at the core of everything we do.

Before exploring how to lead our lives and organizations with purpose, however, we must define the term, which over the past decade has become as confusing as it has become popular.

THE POPULARIZATION OF PURPOSE

In 2009, Simon Sinek's TED Talk, "How Great Leaders Inspire Action," took the Internet by storm. In it, he introduced the "Golden Circle," the idea that individuals and organizations who believe in and prove their reason for existence (their *why),* inspire greater numbers of loyal people to join their movements and buy their products.[1]

Sinek's content was compelling, but his massive audience—28.3 million views online and counting—is as revealing as the talk. People are yearning for purpose in their lives and organizations as never before. Since that talk, countless blog posts, books, and articles have been written about purpose. In fact, some predict it will lead the next economic revolution.

In *The Purpose Economy,* author and social entrepreneur Aaron Hurst presents purpose as *the* new economic driver, which addresses our need to personally develop, find community, and affect something greater than ourselves.[2]

Many argue convincingly that organizations and societies should focus on purpose, though they're often vague about *how* to do this on a practical level—a gap I hope to fill with this book.

PRACTICING PURPOSE TIP

Identify areas in your personal life where you feel a sense of meaning that is more important than yourself. How does it feel? What are you doing?

Like any concept that has the capability of transforming society and the economy, purpose has become a hot topic—a self-help commodity, strategy, and management consulting tactic—but its true meaning sometimes gets lost in the hype. If we're going to define a practical new philosophy of "invisible leadership," we must first define authentic purpose.

To start, purpose is not a trend. The search for purpose is as old as humankind. Our collective search for meaning and purpose has transcended human civilizations and, some argue, is the defining characteristic of the human species.

Viktor Frankl, a Nazi concentration camp survivor and a psychiatrist, was one of the most compelling writers on the human search for purpose. In his book, *Man's Search for Meaning*, he theorized that "striving to find meaning in one's life is the primary motivational force of man." He could make the claim with authority, since a sense of authentic purpose allowed Frankl to endure the worst conditions imaginable.

While imprisoned, he noted that those who had an authentic purpose outside of the camp and themselves were more likely to survive.

The same is true for all of us—both individuals and organizations—whatever level of adversity we face.

Research shows that having a reason to exist that's more important than ourselves or our organizations results in longer life and greater success. I'll cover this transformational research in the next chapter; but first, it is important to explore the origins of purpose.

WHAT IS AUTHENTIC PURPOSE?

The modern conceptualization of purpose can be traced back to the Protestant Reformation of the 1500s.[4] That movement's architect, Martin Luther, saw work as divine. He wrote, "The works of monks and priests, however holy and arduous they may be, do not differ in this light of God from the works of the rustic laborer in the field or the woman going about her household tasks."[5] People are called to do specific work, Luther posited, and cultivating that calling, or authentic purpose, has remained critical to Western society ever since.

Luther's thinking represented a radical departure in the Western world from the traditional view of work as a necessary burden, which had been shaped by philosophers such as Plato and Aristotle.[6] Luther believed our vocations, while offering us employment, should include a duty to others and the world. The Protestant shift in how work was perceived led to a more pronounced division of labor. It shaped the structure of our modern educational system, and it's an important factor in how organizations are structured. The term "purpose economy" might be new, but in a very real sense, the idea that we and everything we do exist for a reason beyond ourselves began with Luther more than five centuries ago.

Despite its long history, defining purpose remains difficult. Steve Taylor, a senior lecturer at the UK's Leeds Beckett University, in a review of the literature on purpose, finds that purpose has innumerable definitions. Some of the most popular use Maslow's classic hierarchy of needs for a definition of purpose largely tied to drives and survival. In this view of purpose, human beings' basic purpose involves procuring food, water, and shelter. According to Taylor's findings, purpose tends to also be defined in terms of a preexisting framework—religion, for example—or personal accumulation of wealth, status, or attention.[7] These definitions of purpose can dominate the thinking but refer mistakenly to "drives" or "goals" and not purpose.

Authentic purpose involves much more.

I draw on positive psychology for a more holistic definition of purpose. Psychologist Carol Ryff, in the 1989 study, "Happiness is Everything, or Is It? Explorations on the Meaning of Psychological Well-being," offers an enduring description of purpose in this realm. Purpose, she writes, comes from "the goals, intentions and sense of directness in life that produce the feeling that one's life is meaningful and act to integrate the various aspects of one's life into a comprehensive whole." Ryff's emphasis on *meaningfulness* is a key distinction from earlier definitions.[8]

Psychologist Corey Keyes in "Authentic Purpose: The Spiritual Infrastructure of Life" added a critical qualifier that draws from Luther and acts as the core of the definition I use in this book. Purpose, Keyes argues, involves two critical elements: a sense of direction in life and a social contribution.

In other words, purpose is not merely personal. We exist to benefit other people. This other-focused qualifier is critical to understanding the concept of authentic purpose.

Through reviewing the literature on purpose, Keyes finds that four types of purpose emerge:

Purpose that is...

- **Aimless but useful:** a purpose that benefits society but doesn't have an associated goal.

- **Aimless and useless:** a purpose that only exists for the sake of an associated goal.

- **Directed but useless:** a purpose with a goal that doesn't benefit other people.

- **Authentic:** a purpose that is both directed and useful for the world.[9]

Keyes's definition—in particular, his insistence that authentic purpose benefits others—informs my own, but he leaves room for a trap that I hope to address in this book. Understanding purpose as a goal that benefits others tempts organizations and individuals to simply copy someone else's purpose. This is what I call "phony purpose," and it's what Purpose Guide Institute founder Jonathan Gustin labeled "default purpose" in a recent interview I conducted with him.

A phony or default purpose is one that another person or organization or the marketplace has described for us. Countless people and organizations embrace default purposes to the detriment of careers, selfhood, organizational health, and economic output.

> **AUTHENTIC PURPOSE: A PERSON OR ORGANIZATION'S GENUINE AND UNIQUE REASON FOR EXISTENCE THAT IS USEFUL TO OTHERS IN SOCIETY.**

Building on Keyes's definition then, while guarding against the temptation of imitation, I define authentic purpose as: *a person or organization's genuine and unique reason for existence that is useful to others in society.*

Genuineness, or authenticity, is critical. An *authentic* purpose is the ultimate differentiator and competitive advantage. No matter who you are, what industry you work in, what you're studying in school, or which organization you run, people can always copy *what you do*, but no one can copy *why you are*.

RESULTS ≠ PURPOSE

Awakening your authentic reason for existence is a vital step toward leading with authentic purpose, but in working with individuals and organizations, I find that people confuse purpose with results, tactics, or strategies—a mistake that undermines their real reason for being.

I saw a case of this sort of drift from authentic purpose recently when I was charged with motivating the sales team of a Fortune 500 engineering and automation firm. I did what I always do to prepare for such talks with sales teams and spent weeks being a "customer" looking to buy an industrial robot. I didn't know much about buying an industrial robot, but I shopped around, downloaded brochures, and reviewed the sales materials and value propositions for the company and its competitors. Here's what they told me.

> PEOPLE CAN ALWAYS COPY WHAT YOU DO, BUT NO ONE CAN COPY WHY YOU ARE.

Competitor A told me it was an industry leader, could increase my profitability and competitiveness, and would provide world-class customer service. Competitor B told me it was an industry leader, could increase my profitability and competitiveness, and would provide world-class customer service. My client, the company that hired me, told me that it was an industry leader, could increase my profitability and competitiveness, and would provide world-class customer service.

What do you notice?

Of course, at the end of my little experiment, I had no clue whom to buy from or why. Maybe the price and product specifications would help, I thought, but no; they were almost identical for all three companies. In fact, after my keynote address, a salesperson said, "You know, Zach, you're right. The technology is all the same." This company was spending hundreds of thousands of dollars on a differentiation strategy that did nothing to differentiate it.

PRACTICING PURPOSE TIP

Start consciously detaching your understanding of personal or organizational purpose from results or return. Now, ask deeper, "What is the purpose of this beyond any 'what' or result?" Do I/we focus more on results or purpose?

As I reflected on my research, though, I remembered a phrase that was plastered on the company's wall, pressed into its logo, and incorporated into its general information. At the end of its mission statement were the most powerful four words I had read in the company's materials: "… for a better world." This was *the* automation company that literally existed, per its stated mission, to better the world.

Where was this purpose in its differentiation strategy? This was why it existed, and which of its rivals could compete with that? None! And yet, when I'd posed as a customer, I never once got a sense of this authentic purpose from its marketing materials, or website.

What a difference it would have made if one of the salespeople I'd spoken to had said, "I love my job because we make the world better. That's our whole purpose. We care about helping people and helping your business deliver its purpose. Oh, and we can also increase your profitability and competitiveness and provide you with world-class customer service, and together, we can be industry leaders."

I would have placed my order right then and there.

As I spoke to the sales force at the company conference, I helped them to flip their value proposition and put their authentic purpose out front. People became visibly more excited about their work. Imagine the child of a salesperson asking, "Hey, what do you *really* do?" And Mom or Dad, who might have had trouble answering last week, now saying, "Well, I help make the world a better place."

Having a purpose that improves the world lights us up. It is a psychological force that activates us and is our ultimate differentiator. The automation firm missed this dynamic for reasons that are all too common. It confused purpose with results. Purpose is not a result. Purpose is not profit or a paycheck. It is not a line on your resume. It is not having friends or college degrees. These are the *results* of purpose.

What do I mean by this? No one ever created a job merely to pay you. Every position you've held, from the part-time teenage post to the serious career, exists to solve some human problem. I thought I painted houses in college for a paycheck. I now realize that I did that job to help people feel better about the spaces where they spent most of their time. If I'd been more in tune with the true purpose of that work, I would have known this from the way customers' faces lit up when we did an excellent job.

Purpose is the reason for your rare and precious existence that betters the world.

Despite what various leaders, coaches, business writers, and others promoting purpose have said lately, it is not something a person or an organization can *do*. You cannot "do" a reason for existence. Purpose isn't a board-retreat exercise that will magically boost sales, fundraise more dollars, or motivate employees. It isn't a quick self-help read that will instantly make you happier. Authentic purpose forces us, as individuals and organizations, to answer the daily questions: Why me? Why here? Why now?

Purpose has become so misunderstood and confused with results and strategy that we should spell out some of the things it *isn't*.

The process of awakening purpose is difficult, but ironically, when companies, organizations, and people embrace a guiding purpose that seeks to better the world beyond their financial success and other results, financial success and results tend to follow.

THE SIX THINGS PURPOSE ISN'T

1. A well-worded statement. Much has been written about wording purpose statements to attract and motivate stakeholders, but if the motivation is just money or success, the statement doesn't reflect true purpose. It's a classic carrot-on-a-stick tactic disguised as a purpose.

2. Obtainable in the future. Purpose is not a future goal or strategic priority; it's time-neutral. It's why you existed twenty years ago and why you will exist in twenty more. If market conditions or life circumstances determine your purpose, it isn't real. For instance, a purpose crafted to attract millennial employees is actually a tactic, not a purpose. A sales goal is not a purpose, and neither is any financial target.

3. **Known.** People *know* mission statements. They can recite them and put them under their e-mail signatures. Purpose, on the other hand, is *believed* and pervades every aspect of behavior and attitude. If, for example, you worked for the automation firm in my example and *believed* you were bettering the world, it would be tough to hate Mondays—but it's easy to *know* a mission statement and wish it was Friday.

4. **A fix-all.** A compelling purpose, like this book, is only a starting point. It will not solve every problem. No one will care why you exist unless you systematically prove it every day to the people who matter.

5. **An exercise.** If purpose were something you could do, every person and organization would do it. As Sinek pointed out, Martin Luther King, Jr. didn't "do" civil rights, he believed in them—and proved it every single day, inspiring others to believe what he believed.

6. **Easy.** If any of this sounds easy, you have misunderstood. Purpose is messy. It involves a descent into your or your organization's soul. It is not a one-day workshop. It means facing down everything not aligned with your reason for being. It requires reimagining your life, leadership, and organization to rebuild something that's authentic to your *why*.

A GROWING NEED FOR THE INVISIBLE LEADER

Why do we so urgently need authentic purpose as a leadership style now?

Gallup conducted more than eighty-thousand interviews in 2014 and 2015 as part of an ongoing study and found that just 13 percent of the world's workers were engaged in their jobs. In the United States, that number was just 32 percent, and the problem didn't only affect low-paid workers. The interviews revealed that 37 percent of leaders and managers also felt disengaged at work. The last statistic is especially troubling, since people on average spend around 35 percent of their waking lives at work.[10] How can the experience be positive for them if even their leaders are disengaged?

PRACTICING PURPOSE TIP

Review the six things purpose is not and your current strategy or thinking around purpose. Identify where misunderstandings have occurred.

Still more disturbing is what happens when these disengaged workers go home. They have partners and friends. They raise children. They buy services and goods. They are our economy, community, and society—and if they're uninspired or even miserable at work, they can be just as flat, unengaged, and detached in all aspects of life.

Despite the rising popularity of purpose as an idea, we continue to face a purpose drought on the ground and among leaders. People in the millennial generation are clamoring for work that's meaningful and will better the world. By 2025, they will account for nearly 75 percent of workers in the US, according to a 2016 study by Deloitte. In the same study, more than 70 percent of millennials indicated that companies' purpose and commitment to a greater good were critical factors in deciding whether or not to work for them.[11]

A spiritual calling and sense of higher purpose was also critical when considering a career for 68 percent of college students surveyed by psychologists Bryan Dik and Ryan Duffy in their book, *Make Your Job a Calling*. In my work in both the private sector and higher education, I see the same attitude manifested among future leaders.[12]

Tomorrow's workers, leaders, and consumers are on to something. Research suggests that purpose not only fulfills and engages people, it can help them live longer—and add longevity to their organizations.

And yet, in studying thousands of managers at organizations ranging from General Electric to the Girl Scouts, Authentic Leadership Institute President Nick Craig and Harvard Professor Scott Snook found that fewer than 20 percent of leaders have a strong sense of their own purpose.[13]

Even fewer can distill it into a concrete statement, and almost none have a concrete plan or method for delivering purpose at the personal or organizational level.

We seem to understand that purpose is important, and growing research shows that it both compels people and acts as the ultimate differentiator. But even smart, successful leaders don't know how to deliver purpose. Without a practical plan for turning purpose into action, for infusing every thought, behavior, and interaction with it, leaders are limiting themselves and their organizations.

The rest of this book will help you remove those limitations by awakening, clarifying, and delivering your authentic purpose.

 PRACTICING PURPOSE EXERCISE

1. Think back to when you felt your work (or school, etc.) was most meaningful to you. Describe that moment in detail. Who was there? Where were you? What were you doing?

2. Outside of any result, goal, or another person's opinion, expectation, or definition, why does what you do exist in the world?

3. In which areas of your organization or life have you seen "default purpose" at work? What are the barriers, if any, to embracing your authentic purpose?

CHAPTER 2

THE POWER OF AUTHENTIC PURPOSE

*The two most important days in your life are the day
you are born and the day you find out why.*

—*Mark Twain*

Purpose is personal to me.

I can still hear the dial tone that was the soundtrack of my first "real" job out of college and vividly recall my manager's incessant advice: "If you keep your finger on the receiver button and don't put the handset down, you can make ten more cold-calls in an hour." I worked in radio-advertising sales—"sold air," as they say in the industry. I got to wear a suit, make good money, and live in a townhouse outside DC with a big-screen television. I could go to happy hours and tell people, "Hey, I'm in advertising." I had every "thing" that drove my decisions up to that point—the title, the money, and the status. It all looked so good to my parents, friends, Facebook connections, and the counselors at my undergraduate university's career center.

The problem? They were all "things." I had no sense of purpose. In short, I was living someone else's life. My decisions up to this point were based solely on results, on the *idea* of a job and career and all that came with it. I was doing what people who didn't know me *told* me I was supposed to be doing; I was living a *default purpose.*

So how did I get there? For starters, I hadn't been asking the right questions. I never asked, "Why?"

When I reflect on my college years, I realize that I knew my authentic purpose very early on. I got involved in various campus activities—and the commonality of all my involvements, and what interested me most, was helping and motivating people to achieve their visions for themselves. But like many college students (and people in general), that purpose wasn't cultivated to become a viable "job" or "career." Let's just say that researching and consulting on purpose and meaningfulness weren't listed in a course catalog. So I stuffed this idea deep down inside for the sake of the practical. I started comparing myself with others who seemed to know "what" they wanted to do with their lives, and I ultimately faked my way into that advertising job. For the record, I have

WHEN YOU LIVE BY RESULTS, YOU DIE BY RESULTS.

nothing against advertising sales. I was fairly good at it and enjoyed the rush of it all. My unsettledness in that job had nothing to do with the job—it had everything to do with a lack of purpose *in* the job.

What happened to me is precisely what I've seen happen to both people and organizations who focus solely on results, on "things" to be achieved. They tend to drift toward the conventional, fall into a default state, and lose their ultimate differentiator and competitive advantage—their purpose.

The culture of the organization I worked with in that first job was as results-obsessed as I had been in college. In our meetings, all we talked about were targets and sales goals. We didn't talk about helping potential customers build better businesses (which was why our jobs existed in the first place). As a result, the team had built a flimsy foundation, which could be crumbled by one bad financial quarter.

I see this in organizations and individuals I work with. When you live by results, you die by results.

Lucky for me, in the midst of my searching, I met someone who would dramatically alter the trajectory of my life—an unlikely character who opened my eyes to the power of purpose in action.

THE CAB DRIVER WHO CHANGED MY LIFE

Sometimes in that first year I would leave work for one or two hours at a time and sit in a park outside Reagan National Airport, in Washington, DC. I remember watching the planes overhead, thinking, is this all there is? Is this what "working" is all about? Lost in thought one day I noticed that a cab had pulled up next to me. The driver got out and lit a cigarette; he asked how I was doing.

PRACTICING PURPOSE TIP

Explicitly stating a reason for existence and keeping it visible (even if it is in development) can harmonize energy in organizations and life.

"Is it the weekend yet?" I replied, embarrassed a moment later when I remembered that it was only Monday. (It is astounding to think about how many people live for two-sevenths of their lives.)

"Hey, are you okay?" he asked, looking genuinely concerned.

I grumbled something about just trying to make it through the week and asked how work was going for him.

"It's amazing," he said, putting out the cigarette. "You can't beat it." I must have looked shocked. He continued, "I mean, I get to talk to new people from around the world every half-hour and drive a car around the nation's capital. It really is amazing." For some reason I expected this cab driver to hate his job, but he loved it.

He gave a big grin as he got back into his cab.

"Maybe I should be a cab driver." I laughed to myself.

After the interaction, I realized that I was emotionally drawn by how he talked about his work. He seemed genuinely passionate about his job. And then I realized something: he didn't talk about *what* he did. He talked about *why* he did it.

He was a traveling conversationalist who just happened to drive cabs. That was the moment it all clicked for me. Everything we do has a reason for existence that is bigger than us. And when we focus on and communicate that reason, we compel others.

I have noted this phenomenon in my work and research again and again. The most extraordinary people I meet are the ones who do ordinary things with an extraordinary perspective. That extraordinary perspective is rooted in purpose.

The interaction with the cab driver led me to leave my first job out of college—and ultimately is the reason I am writing this book. After advertising, I worked for almost nine years in higher education. My mission was simple: to make sure none of our future leaders ended up like me. It was in academia, though, where I discovered that our society suffers from a purpose drought, especially when it comes to how we educate our future workers.

THE MOST EXTRAORDINARY PEOPLE I MEET ARE THE ONES WHO DO ORDINARY THINGS WITH AN EXTRAORDINARY PERSPECTIVE.

One of the more powerful revelations about this "miseducation" came during a session I led for students who hadn't declared their majors yet. I asked the audience a simple question: "*Why* are you in college?" A student in the front row teared up. Taken aback, I asked her why the question made her emotional.

"No one ever asked me that before," she said.

She had been in college for almost a year, and not one educator had asked her *why* she was there. Having no idea why she was in college—and, therefore, no solid narrative to base her decisions on, she felt empty and directionless. I realized then that the need for purpose is fundamentally human and decided to dedicate the rest of my life to empowering purposeful people and building purposeful organizations.

I focused my doctoral studies on organizational learning, performance, and change—specifically studying meaningful work and purpose—and began to work with a wide variety of organizations in nearly every industry.

PRACTICING PURPOSE TIP

Do you motivate yourself and people with "things" or with purpose and meaning? Purpose and meaning are more powerful and sustainable.

Through my research I've found that a purposeful approach, which I will outline in detail later in the book, requires a radical change in our thinking. This mindset shift is counter to how the world has taught us to view our lives, work, and organizations: as a series of "things" to be achieved and acquired.

While results can push people temporarily, purpose gives them something to strive for, and as we'll explore in the research that follows, purpose is *the* crucial element in motivation, performance, and health for individuals and organizations.

WIRED FOR PURPOSE

In 1944, psychologists Fritz Heider and Marianne Simmel designed a simple animation that lasted two and a half minutes. Large and small black triangles, a black circle, and a simple rectangle moved randomly against a white background. They showed the clip to 114 randomly chosen subjects and asked them to write down what happened in the picture.

The results were astounding. In all but one case, subjects described the shapes as animated or live human beings.[1] They attached emotions, intentions, gender, and intricate emotional story-lines to the shapes and how they moved. The large black triangle moving near the smaller one became a "bully," the circle was a "child," and the rectangle entered into complex "relationships."

The landmark study reflected the human brain's natural inclination to attach meaning to the chaos of our lives and work, to find an overarching narrative—a purpose. But perhaps more compelling, it showed that as human beings, our brains are wired to find purpose and meaning in whatever we do. And if people can find compelling meaning in shapes, imagine the meaning they must attach to the complex human organizations we find ourselves part of every day.

In my own work, I regularly show this animation, and whether the audience consists of college students or organizational leaders, the results are the same. Every participant attaches meaning and purpose to the animation—and they're all different interpretations. We all search for purpose.

During my graduate studies, I read an article in which Ali Binazir, a medical doctor and professor at Harvard, attempted to quantify the chances of any of us being born in the first place.

After calculating for things like the chances of your biological parents meeting on the planet and the chances of each of their parents meeting (and so on) since the beginning of time, he determined that you had about a one in four-hundred-quadrillion chance of even existing.[2] That means that, according to the dictionary definition of a miracle, you are a miracle. Every person is—and so are organizations, since they're composed of people.

It's not a surprise, then, that the most important question of our lives and work becomes: Why me, why here, why now? How do we justify this rare existence? How do we justify how we spend our time? What story do we attach our lives to?

In the absence of explicitly stated answers to those key questions, people (and organizations) inevitably make up their own as they go. It follows that our actions and decisions can sometimes seem random. For example, when I show the Heider and Simmel animation and explicitly tell the audience a clear story-line, people spontaneously fit their interpretations into the larger narrative.

This is how purpose acts—as a grand narrative for our lives and work. When we state an authentic purpose very clearly, it becomes the overarching story of our lives. It pulls our actions, decisions, and attitudes in one direction. It acts like a magnetic north pole. Everything aligns with the larger purpose—but take away the explicitly stated reason for existence, and chaos tends to ensue. For example, organizations without a clear authentic purpose leave stakeholders to invent one. The result can be hundreds or even thousands of purposes, some differing only in marginal ways, but others, inevitably, at odds and working against each other.

One of the most prominent sources of workplace conflict, I've found, involves conflicting purposes. In education, when students don't have a clear purpose, they don't perform as well as they could. An exam is just an exam versus part of the larger narrative of life.

IT'S NOT A SURPRISE, THEN, THAT THE MOST IMPORTANT QUESTION OF OUR LIVES AND WORK BECOMES: WHY ME, WHY HERE, WHY NOW?

On the other hand, a clearly stated authentic purpose harmonizes energy. Actions, attitudes, behaviors, thoughts, policies, and decisions are all oriented toward the larger reason for existence. Because we are wired for purpose, research has convincingly found that the ones who follow this invisible leader may be more likely to succeed in the new "purpose economy."

Awakening and delivering purpose will be the vital leadership skill of the coming decades.

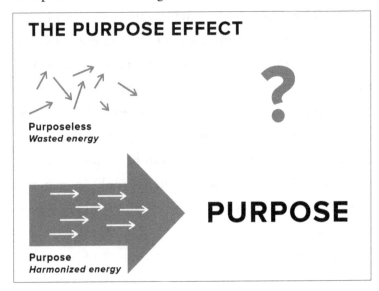

From new college graduates to CEOs, learning to foster this invisible leader is critical. Doing so means changing our mental models of what we think motivates human beings and shifting our view away from the results and the *whats* to the cultivation of firm *whys*—the grand narratives that provide meaning and align our lives and our organizations.

RESULTS DON'T DRIVE PEOPLE, PURPOSE DOES

Research since the 1950s has demonstrated that people's desire to work, study, or better themselves rests on motivations much deeper than financial security. In one landmark study from that decade, sociologists Nancy Morse and Robert Weiss looked for insight into why people work.

They pioneered the "lottery question," which you've probably heard of, since it's still frequently asked today: "If you won the lottery, would you continue to work?" The answer, overwhelmingly, was yes. Morse and Weiss's results showed a critical error in the dominant thinking about work, one still made three-quarters of a century later: that people work primarily for money. Morse and Weiss's interviews with a random sample of more than four hundred employees revealed that work provided much more than just pay. "In fact, even if they had enough money to support themselves, they would still want to work," the sociologists wrote. "Working gives them a feeling of being tied into the larger society, of having something to do, of having a purpose in life."[3]

Their results have been replicated many times. In *Man's Search for Meaning*, Viktor Frankl referenced a Johns Hopkins University study in which 7,948 students at forty-eight colleges were asked what they considered important. Only 16 percent of respondents said that making a lot of money was important, while 78 percent said that finding purpose and meaning was important.[4]

More recently, author and sociologist Reginald Bibby surveyed more than ten thousand new workers in various industries about what they thought critical in a good job. Most rated interesting work, a sense of accomplishment, and adding to people's lives or to some larger purpose as far more important than pay or job security.[5]

In my own research, I reviewed many of the major studies done in the last seventy-five years on why people commit to an organization or movement. I discovered that the weakest form of commitment was transactional (benefits and pay), and the strongest was emotional (connection to an organization, leader, or life direction). One of the key ways to generate emotional commitment, my research also showed, is by cultivating meaning and purpose.

So why do our organizations and educational systems still focus so heavily on results—benefits, paychecks, bonuses, titles, suits—as the chief motivators?

It's time that we listen not just to the research but to our workers and ourselves. We are all *wired* for purpose, and we yearn to be compelled—not just driven.

THE PURPOSE EFFECT

Purpose might even help us live longer.

For example, in a 2015 study of more than 136,000 men and women, Dr. Randy Cohen found that when people indicated a clear purpose in their lives and work—one outside of themselves—they had a 23 percent lower mortality rate and 19 percent fewer cardiovascular events.[6] The National Institutes of Health found that having a sense of purpose can add up to seven years to a person's life.[7] It also makes sense that organizations embracing purpose would also last longer and be healthier, just like the individuals who comprise them.

Purpose sharpens our minds too. A 2014 Gallup and Healthways study found that a sense of purpose doubles the likelihood of learning something new each day, and Richard Leider in his book, *The Power of Purpose*, found that a sense of purpose yields a 42 percent increase in the experience of regular contentment.[8, 9]

So what is the answer to questions like these: What will make our employees happy? What will make people emotionally commit to work? What will make us happier in life? The answer may simply be: discovering a purpose beyond yourself.

Purpose, like other sources of happiness, has a way of quietly solving a wide variety of problems. Its benefits are contagious. According to a study by Imperative and New York University, purposeful employees were 64 percent more likely to be fulfilled, 50 percent more likely to get promoted, and 47 percent more likely to tell the story of their employers.[10, 11] Regarding the engagement crisis, a 2014 Gallup study found that employees with a clear sense of purpose beyond self were four times more likely to be engaged in their work.[11] Employees with purpose can be your most powerful recruiters, whether you lead a for-profit organization or a nonprofit movement. If they're attached to the purpose, people tell the story because it becomes *their* story.

In their effort to scientifically validate an instrument for measuring meaning in work, psychologists Michael Steger, Bryan Dik, and Ryan Duffy found that workers who experienced their work as meaningful and serving a greater purpose left their jobs at lower rates, were absent fewer times, and demonstrated greater involvement in the organization.[12]

Why does purpose seem so much more powerful than traditional motivation tactics and results? When we have a purpose that's bigger than ourselves, it's often impossible to complete in a single lifetime. It inspires a never-ending striving. While motivation pushes us, purpose pulls.

PURPOSE PULLS

"Humans are pushed by drives," Viktor Frankl wrote, "... but pulled by meaning." The classic motivation tactics of our society focus on pushing. You'll see the language in most business articles and self-help books: *discover what drives you, push yourself to the next level.*

But there is a reason that we have tow trucks and not push trucks. Basic physics tells us that when you push, there is one component of force that adds to the weight of the body and so adds friction. When you pull, the vertical component of the force is against the weight of the body and the overall friction diminishes. It is, in the simplest terms, easier to pull than to push.

Purpose works the same way in psychological terms, pulling us forward. Classic results-focused motivation tactics give us short pushes, but the attendant friction inevitably slows us down and it doesn't last. This may be why self-help books are so popular and new management fads so quickly adopted by organizations. We're all looking for a quick fix. Often, though, we end up right back where we were.

An authentic purpose, however, can pull us through difficulties, keep us focused, and lessen friction in personal and organizational life.

PRACTICING PURPOSE TIP

Use purpose in difficult times to "pull" yourself and people you serve through.

This elementary physics lesson provides us an example of why most motivation tactics fail or are short lived. We try to push people by offering rewards, big salaries, good grades, or flashy perks. This is difficult, expensive *pushing*, and its benefits are often temporary at best.

Purpose inspires self-transcendence, which lasts. Self-transcendence can best and simply be defined as the phenomenon that occurs when one's behaviors, actions, or decisions are oriented toward an object outside of the self. In the workplace, studies have shown, one of the most powerful objects for such transcendence is an organizational purpose that serves others beyond the bounds of the organization.

In their book, *Make Your Job a Calling*, psychology professors Bryan Dik and Ryan Duffy found when employees have a "transcendent summons" (a larger purpose outside the organization), they are more committed to their jobs, intrinsically motivated, engaged, and satisfied.[13]

Creating an organizational culture with a compelling purpose inspires self-transcendence and pulls employees along, building engagement and loyalty. Because of its global nature (an idea I'll investigate later), an authentic purpose is never completely satisfied, so the striving and pulling will always be there.

PURPOSEFUL PEOPLE DRIVE ORGANIZATIONAL RESULTS

Purposeful people, pulled by meaning and self-transcendence, drive organizational results. Organizations are simply individuals who come together to accomplish something, so it makes sense: when people are pulled by meaning and purpose, organizations experience results. In *Built to Last*, Jim Collins found that companies whose leaders embrace a higher society-bettering purpose outperform the market and their peers by an average of 6:1.[14]

Those companies also, on average, experience growth rates three times those of their competitors. Unilever is a good example. Its brands with clearly communicated societal purposes—household names like Comfort, Dove, and Ben & Jerry's—are growing faster than the rest of the company's portfolio. In an article I recently cowrote with colleagues from the social enterprise Gone Adventurin, Unilever CEO Paul Polman said, "Our sustainable-living brands are growing

30 percent faster than the rest of our business and delivered nearly half of our total growth in 2015."

Because purpose emotionally compels us, people are more likely to buy a product connected to a social movement. Dove changed nothing about its soap when it sought to respond to the societal pressures on women regarding body image; instead, it sharply defined its overarching purpose as "helping women feel better about their bodies." Because Dove stated a purpose that was more important than itself, it inspired employees and consumers to join the movement. The result was a $1.5 billion increase in sales in a decade. The soap is the same, but its story and narrative transformed.

Other studies have shown similar results. In his research, former Procter & Gamble marketing director Jim Stengel found that purpose-driven brands performed ten times better than others in similar categories, and they grew at a significantly faster rates than the overall market.[15] In "The Business Case for Purpose," EY Beacon Institute and *The Harvard Business Review* found that 58 percent of companies with a clear global purpose experienced growth of greater than 10 percent, while only 42 percent of non-purpose-driven companies did.[16]

The evidence shows similar results for nonprofits, educational institutions, and other movements and endeavors. When we make the leader of an organization or movement its authentic purpose, results follow. Clearly, then, it will be beneficial to cultivate this invisible leader by shifting our mindset as leaders.

WE CAN LEARN A PURPOSEFUL MINDSET

Like any new way of thinking, a sense of purpose doesn't just happen. You can't go out and get it. It can't be ordered or bought. Awakening purpose takes the same practice and patience as any new habit or skill, which is why I'm writing this book. But can a purposeful mindset be learned? A recent study suggests that it can.

Psychologist David Yeager and his colleagues wanted to know whether purpose could lead to greater academic success among high school students. They designed a simple thirty-minute reading and writing exercise, in which under-performing students logged onto an online platform and read an article containing quotes from actual students, conveying this message: *high school could help them do something that matters in the world.* The researchers wanted to see if students would perform better on mundane tasks if they saw a purpose beyond self.

The stories by students who had gone *before* those in the study, detailed the impact high school had on their self-image, their view of the world, and their personal-development goals. The 338 students reading the quotes then wrote short testimonials for *future* students, describing how high school helped them to develop and to impact the world.

Please note: the researchers did not ask about the grades students got, how they passed classes, or how they succeeded with particular teachers.

After a few months, the students who participated saw a .2 percent average increase in GPA.[17] That might not sound significant, but a .2 percent increase can be the difference between a B and an A, between getting into a particular college or not, between a scholarship or full tuition bills. The boost in grades didn't follow a discussion of grades (a result) but an awareness of and commitment to a purpose beyond self. When students could attach their immediate task to a grander narrative of the life they wanted to lead, results followed.

Most important, the study showed that a purposeful mindset can be learned. This is what the rest of this book will explore: How do we learn to lead with authentic purpose? How do we learn to put the *why* before the *what*?

 PRACTICING PURPOSE EXERCISE

1. Make a list of how you motivate others in your organization or yourself. Now, after you write down an item, identify whether it is a thing (T) or a purpose (P). Do you have more Ts or Ps? Where are areas you can work on to be more purpose-led?

   Keep these in mind as we move forward in the book.

2. Think of a moment where a purpose beyond any result or thing pulled you through a difficult situation. How did you stay aligned with that purpose?

CHAPTER 3

INVISIBLE LEADERSHIP

*Leaders and followers are both following the
invisible leader—the common purpose.*

—*Mary Parker Follett*

The University of Colorado Buffaloes finished the 1988
football season with an eight-and-four record, then lost in
the Freedom Bowl. Two years later, the team finished with
eleven wins and clinched the NCAA championship. Traditional leadership theories don't explain what happened
between 1988 and 1990. The same coach was with the team
for more than five years. Players remained at relatively consistent skill levels, and the Buffaloes organization made no
major changes. The "what" of the organization remained
essentially the same.

The sea change came in the "why," the team's purpose.

A year before CU embarked on the 1990 run that would
lead to a national championship, its star quarterback, a
vibrant twenty-year-old named Sal Aunese began showing up
to practice in visible pain and distress, sometimes vomiting

uncontrollably. The team checked its star quarterback, the future of the program, into the hospital.

The diagnosis was inoperable stomach cancer. Already, it had spread throughout Sal's body. Doctors gave him six months to live. Sal vowed to fight. He promised to play football again. He showed up to his team's practices and delivered emotional talks to the team when he could. His teammates said that often, when Sal tried to motivate them, he became too emotional to speak. The fact that he was there, devoted as ever, was incredibly inspiring.

In the buildup to the Buffaloes' turning-point 1989 season, Sal vowed that he would live to see every matchup. Before games, the entire team kneeled and pointed up to where Sal was sitting in the stands. They were pointing at their reason for playing, a purpose bigger than all of them— to fight for Sal.

Sadly, Sal died from complications related to his cancer midway through the 1989 season, but his courage and his fight lived on. His impact on the athletes grew more powerful, even as Sal was no longer physically present.

Over time, as depicted vividly in the ESPN documentary *The Gospel According to Mac*, players put personal goals and egos aside to create a shared, authentic *why* that would *pull* them through the next two years, until they won the national championship.[1]

"The bus sort of drove itself," said Gary Barnett, a quarterbacks and fullbacks coach for the Buffaloes, in an interview with Boulder's *Daily Camera* newspaper.[2]

Sal became more than a person. He grew into an idea, a purpose, a reason—and that purpose bonded the group and ignited what head coach Bill McCartney later called a "rally cry." That rally cry was an authentic purpose greater than any one player or leader, greater than any one coach. In fact, the leader of the Colorado Buffaloes was invisible and not a person at all. And, many argue it was the invisible force that pulled them through the 1989 season and into the 1990 championship.

This is the power of the invisible leader.

By reframing our understanding of leadership and learning the skills to cultivate authentic purpose—life's most compelling leader—we, too, can build gritty, resilient, striving lives and organizations.

WHAT IS INVISIBLE LEADERSHIP?

The term invisible leadership dates to an article written in 1928 by Mary Parker Follett, the famed social worker, philosopher, and management consultant. She called for a redefinition of leadership, from the classic *power-over* mentality to a *power-with* mentality. Follett envisioned a leadership style less about coercion, command, and control, and more about freedom. She implored organizations to create environments where people would be free to think, behave, and choose the best courses of action to accomplish a common purpose. In her paradigm, people are not commanded by a person.

Instead, as she said, ". . . both leaders and followers follow the invisible leader—the common purpose."[3]

PRACTICING PURPOSE TIP

Apart from any one person, identify the idea, reason, or purpose that is most powerful to you or people in an organization you're a part of.

When we put authentic purpose at the core of our lives and organizations, we lead with the opposite of coercion. We lead with freedom, allowing people to be pulled together by a common reason for existence. Leading with authentic purpose means cultivating an idea, awakening a reason, and crystallizing it. When you do that, as a coach of that Buffaloes' football team noted, the bus drives itself. The invisible leader inspires and helps us strive, not because we have to but because we deeply *want* to. We want to fulfill a purpose so much that no barrier is too big to overcome and a shared authentic purpose becomes more important than ourselves or our organization.

Leadership scholars Gill Hickman and Georgia Sorenson, in their article "Unmasking Leadership," describe purpose as existing in the space between people and the achievement of their shared dreams. They liken this transitional space to the blue notes in jazz, the in-between notes that make the whole piece come together. Invisible leadership, they propose, exists when the dedication to a common, compelling, and deeply held common reason for existence is a group's primary motivating force.[4]

Exploring invisible leadership further, Hickman and Sorenson surveyed twenty-one high-performing companies and nonprofits. All had a deeply held common destiny, or sense of calling, that illuminated and aligned people's values and beliefs and became the key ingredient in the organization's financial and social success. This shared purpose was a primary reason people wanted to work at the organizations, and it was the reason they stayed. Hickman and Sorenson's research showed that, at these organizations, purpose proved more powerful than any person's charisma—a dynamic they began to call "the charisma of purpose."

PRACTICING PURPOSE TIP

Align people's (and your own) personal values and vision for their life with the broader purpose and vision. Assess what those personal visions are.

In the following chapters I'll present a roadmap for cultivating this invisible leader in your life, organization, or movement. The process requires awakening purpose, clarifying it, and ultimately, delivering and proving it. But before we redefine leadership in terms of authentic purpose, it's important to consider the traditional philosophies that shaped the dominant leadership paradigms and the need they leave unfulfilled.

We are taught through socialization to view leadership as commanding, controlling, and managing. Take a look at our political landscape, media outlets, and biggest companies, and you will see the same leadership theories that Mary Parker Follett criticized in 1928. Coercion, power, control, and manipulation commonly dominate. However, as we saw in chapter 2, motivating people by commanding and controlling them is contrary to human nature; it's a style of leadership that neglects what actually motivates and inspires people: meaning and purpose.

PRACTICING PURPOSE TIP

Become aware of what style of leadership you currently exhibit or is prevalent in your organization. What are the limitations?

The same is true in our own lives. When we try to rigorously control our lives and plans, we leave no room for freedom and creativity. We begin stifling ourselves and our potential for success. People want inspiration. We want to be compelled, and not by another's will or through the manipulations of rewards, benefits, and carrots that may push us forward but only temporarily.

On the topic of leadership, Amazon lists more than three hundred thousand (and, I guess, one more now) titles. Leadership is what shapes our companies, communities, and countries; yet, one of the most important concepts in human civilization is also one of the most poorly misunderstood.

DOMINANT THEORIES OF LEADERSHIP

I teach a course at Colorado State University called "Leading with Authentic Purpose" for college sophomores with various majors and diverse backgrounds. On the first day, I start with a simple exercise—one you can try now.

Think back to the first time in your life you learned what or who a leader was. Try to describe the experience in detail. Who was there, what was the situation? And how did you know that the person was a leader?

Students' most common examples include the peer who always won playing tag on the playground, appointed hall monitors in grade school or parents and older siblings at home. They describe people in positional power. Leaders are labeled as parent, teacher, monitor, captain—almost always in an appointed role with freely given power. There's usually little questioning of why the leaders have this power; often it seems arbitrary. Some students also talk about group projects in which people who appear to have more expertise or experience become leaders.

The scenarios students relate, like the ones I bet you're remembering now, involve commanding and controlling others or being an "expert." Those earliest experiences with leadership are formative, the first steps in a lifetime of viewing leadership as primarily about power and position. The traits students describe in my course are the same ones that have dominated the major leadership theories guiding our lives and organizations for more than a century.

In Peter Northouse's expansive book, *Leadership: Theory and Practice*, he reviews nearly every leadership theory in human history, tracing the concept's historical evolution. Historically, he writes, we have adopted a trait-based approach to leadership, where things like intelligence, charisma, appearance, and position make a leader, charged with motivating followers in a top-down relationship.

However, the emergent view of leadership is process-based. In this model, Northouse says, leadership occurs in the context of interactions between leaders and followers.[5] Leadership is available to everyone in a particular context. Leading with authentic purpose, or the notion of an invisible leader, falls within a process conceptualization of leadership because it focuses on the space between people.

Leading with authentic purpose is a departure from the dominant paradigm, but to appreciate how it advances leadership theory, it will help to briefly look at the prevailing historical models—elements of which will look familiar to anyone who's ever gone to school, held a job, joined a club, or lived with a family.

Much of our current understanding of, and socialization around, what leadership is and who can be a leader is derived from historical conceptualizations and how we come to "learn" leadership. Reading the following descriptions, ask if you can see yourself or others in these perspectives. How do you "see" leadership? This self-awareness is important to developing an alternative mindset. This list was created by drawing on the descriptions and classifications formulated by author and educator Kendra Cherry in her 2016 article, "The Eight Major Leadership Theories."[6]

1. **Great-man theories**. These theories assume that the capacity for leadership is inherent and that great leaders are born, not made. Great leaders are portrayed as heroic, mythic, and destined to rise when needed. The term is "great-man" because at one time, leadership was thought of as a primarily male quality, especially military leadership. Great-man theories are prevalent in our society today, including in our political and economic systems.

2. **Trait-based theories**. Trait-based theories assume that some people inherit qualities that make them better suited to leadership than others. Trait theory has often identified certain personality or behavioral characteristics shared by "good leaders." This, however, makes it difficult to explain to people without those qualities that they are not leaders.

3. **Contingency theories**. Contingency theories of leadership focus on the variables that arise in a particular time and place to determine which style of leadership is best suited to the situation. No one leadership style is best, since a style's effectiveness is *contingent* upon the situation. This means that

we judge leaders based on how they respond in particular situations.

4. **Situational theories**. Similar to contingency theories, situational theories propose that leaders choose the best course of action and the most effective style based upon situational variables. Situational leadership can be taught, its adherents assert, and they theorize that different styles of leadership are appropriate for different types of decision making. Many models and process maps have been created to aid in situational leadership.

5. **Behavioral theories**. These theories posit that great leaders are made and not born. They are, as you might guess, rooted in the psychological discipline of behaviorism. They focus on the actions of leaders, not on mental qualities or internal states. People can learn specific behaviors that will make them leaders, according to behavioral theorists.

6. **Participative leadership theories.** These suggest that the ideal leadership style takes the input of others into account. Leaders encourage the participation of and contributions from group members. They help group members feel relevant and committed to the decision-making process. Leaders, however, retain the right to allow or reject others' input.

7. **Transactional theories.** This category includes management theories focusing on the role of supervision in management and group performance. Leadership relies on a system of rewards and punishments. Managerial theories are often used in business, where employees are rewarded for success and punished for failure.

8. **Relationship theories.** These theories focus on transformation and are concerned with the connections formed between leaders and followers. Leaders motivate and inspire by helping people see the importance and greater good of a task. Transformational leaders are focused on performance and want group members to reach their individual potential.

Now for the radical departure from these theories. Invisible leadership asserts that the best leaders aren't people at all. It removes people, positions, and power from the mix and rests on the importance of cultivating a compelling, common *purpose* as the most powerful leader.

> **INVISIBLE LEADERSHIP ASSERTS THAT THE BEST LEADERS AREN'T PEOPLE AT ALL.**

A NEW DEFINITION: PURPOSEFUL LEADERSHIP

Of the theories discussed, relationship theories are closest to the idea of leading with authentic purpose, the invisible leader. Like the other theory bases, though, relationship theories leave a gap, which invisible leadership fills. All the historical theories stipulate that leaders must be trained or educated in a particular style of leadership if they are to lead. They focus on the performance of specific tasks and require one person or a group of people to wield power over another.

Purposeful leadership, or leadership that awakens and instills a common purpose, levels the playing field. It's the same for the factory worker, the CEO, and that cab driver I met in the DC park. The organization's authentic purpose wields the true power over individuals in this theory, or more accurately, it empowers them.

FOR THE PURPOSES OF THIS BOOK, I DEFINE LEADERSHIP AS:

The ongoing process of discovering, enacting, and delivering an authentic personal or organizational purpose, a reason for existence, for the benefit of society. The process must, through relationships, cultivate an environment that allows individuals to discover their personal visions and connect them to a higher purpose for collective action.

How do we do this? How do we cultivate authentic purpose as a leadership philosophy? Invisible leadership starts with awakening purpose. Developing and teaching a purposeful mindset by focusing on the greater good and identifying the problem we exist to solve is critical.

It's then necessary to clarify this purpose, clearly stating our reason for existence, keeping it at the front and center of everything we do and say and in all choices and behaviors. Finally, the goal is to deliver purpose consistently through integrity, values, and experiences designed to prove it to stakeholders.

Purposeful leadership invites freedom and accessibility. It allows everyone who believes in the bigger purpose to be a leader. Belief is central to the framework of the rest of this book, which will teach you to awaken, clarify, and deliver purpose in organizations and in life and also to *believe* in it. Belief is incredibly powerful and quite different from knowledge. When we believe something, we feel it in our core—mind, body, and soul. A belief in a bigger purpose is the most powerful belief of all and, as the University of Colorado Buffaloes can attest, results in amazing accomplishments.

As I mentioned in the introduction, I will focus on three beliefs in the rest of this book:

1. The belief that you and your work (both the individual's and the organization's) matters.

2. The individual and shared belief in a bigger, other-centered purpose—why you do what you do.

3. The belief in proving your purpose consistently.

PRACTICING PURPOSE EXERCISE

Think back to the first time in your life when you encountered a leader. Who was it? Where was it? How did they become a leader? Now, reflect on how this understanding has shaped how you lead your life or organization.

PART II

AWAKENING PURPOSE

CHAPTER 4

HOW HAVE YOU CHANGED THE WORLD TODAY?

Our deepest fear is not that we are inadequate; our
deepest fear is that we are powerful beyond measure. It
is our light, not our darkness, that most frightens us.

—*Marianne Williamson*

How have you changed the world today?

Whatever day you're reading this, whatever the time, take a moment and ask yourself: How have I changed the planet since waking up?

If you're having trouble answering, you're not alone. I ask this question regularly of everyone I work with—teenagers, college students, CEOs, salespeople, and employees in various industries. Typically, I'm greeted with awkward silence and maybe a few eye rolls. People automatically think this is some sentimental, idealistic exercise. But I believe, and research shows, it's one of the most important questions any person or organization can ask.

We have been socialized to believe that we don't matter, that we're too small or our jobs and organizations don't exist to change the world.

The sad difficulty of answering this short question was highlighted for me recently when a colleague and I worked with a therapeutic-recreation department at a children's hospital. The department's mission is to help make kids' (some with terminal diagnoses) lives better. The doctors, nurses, and assistants do this by pairing children with in-room and out-of-room activities like board games and outdoor recreation. Some of the doctors and nurses in the room at my event that day actually helped to start the department.

And I asked, as I always do: *How have you changed the world today?*

After five minutes of silence, the doctors, nurses, and other caregivers could not answer. This group of amazing people undertakes a wide range of creative measures to alleviate pain, spark interest, and bring some joy into the lives of sick children—but still they struggled to answer this fundamental question. Ironically, my then-business partner and I were there to help mediate conflict and do team building.

But the staff already had the best team builder within them, the common purpose of improving children's lives. They had forgotten that they mattered. And to awaken purpose, the belief that we and what we do matters is critical and can help us be more fulfilled and productive.

THE NEED FOR A PURPOSEFUL MINDSET

After that day, I started to wonder: If these remarkable care-givers I worked with couldn't answer the question, who can? We have been socialized to believe that only certain people in certain fields, with a certain amount of power or money, can change the world. For organizations, it seems as though changing the world is reserved only for social entrepreneurs and start-ups.

PRACTICING PURPOSE TIP

Focus on the greater good of all tasks and use your imagina-tion to trace the impact of your daily actions, decisions, and thoughts.

This type of thinking is a trap. Every person, in any organization, changes the world whether we acknowledge it or not. Acknowledging our capacity is the first step toward developing a purposeful mindset. I think the false idea that we can't create big change in small, everyday ways stems from the dominant conceptualizations of leadership covered in the last chapter. When we define impact in such limited terms, we disinvite nearly everyone from changing the world, even though they change it every day.

THE SUMMER JOB THAT CHANGED A LIFE

Early in graduate school, I got an email from someone I thought I had never met. I don't quite remember exactly what it said, but it went something like this: "Zach, I saw on Facebook that you've gone into higher education," she wrote. "I wanted to thank you for getting me to where I am right now." She either wants something, I thought, or she has the wrong Zach. I wrote back, politely explaining that I didn't know her.

"It was July of 2004," she replied. "I was a first-year student at an orientation program at James Madison University in Virginia. There was a guy in a purple shirt with a gold name tag with a last name that sounded like 'Mercutio' from *Romeo and Juliet.* He veered off a path and said to me, 'Hey, how's it going?' It was you, I know it."

There was no way around it. I was a leader for the university's new student orientation that summer. She had the right Zach, but I still didn't remember her. I told her to call. On the phone, she said that she had just gotten engaged to someone she met at work, where she spent 40 to 50 percent of her waking life, and she had been reflective lately on how she got here. She went on to explain that her partner, colleagues, career, and much of the rest of her life could be traced back to that Zach Mercurio guy saying "Hey, how's it going?" I was leveled and I asked her to explain.

That day on campus when I said hello she was considering withdrawing from the university. Apparently, that was her state of mind when I walked over (I don't remember any of this) and said, "Hey, how's it going?" "Not well," she said. She didn't know what to do with her life. She didn't know what to major in, and she thought maybe college wasn't for her.

Apparently I asked, "If I were to give you a bunch of money, what would you do with your day?" She loved to write, she said. I told her that my shift was ending and offered to introduce her to a journalism advisor, since I was heading by the journalism department on my way out. I dropped her off there and that was the last time we talked, until that e-mail.

The entire conversation I had with her that day at her orientation program lasted about two minutes (again, I remember none of it), but she said that reflecting on her life years later in New York, she realized it was our two-minute conversation that got her where she was. She was working as an assistant editor at a major magazine, living in New York City. If I hadn't said hello and taken her to that journalism advisor, she said she would have dropped out of college.

Instead, she learned that journalism was a viable career path and ended up lining up an internship at the magazine where she would soon work. Talking to me put her on the path to becoming a journalist and getting a job she loved at the place where she met her future husband. If she had kids someday, she thought, it would be a result of staying in college and studying journalism—and of talking to me.

That is what I mean by changing the world. Four words changed the trajectory of a human being's entire life.

I had thought of my work that summer as *just* a summer job. I didn't realize why it existed until five years after I stopped doing it, when I got that email.

On the first day of that job, I was handed a big binder with the scripts I had to follow, the times I had to start, and the color shirt I had to wear. Imagine the difference it would have made if, instead, my boss had said, "Welcome! This job exists to potentially change the trajectory of human beings' entire lives in a single conversation."

PRACTICING PURPOSE TIP

Focus on and seek out the stories of people you serve.

It's safe to say my alarm clock would have looked a lot different. I would have considered the potential conversations in every moment and complained far less, knowing that each conversation was potentially a life-changing, world-changing event.

What if we structured organizations and teams around the idea that they are authentically changing the world every day? What if we led with this sense of global purpose and believed we exist to change the world? When you actually believe that you matter, it's difficult to imagine not being motivated or inspired.

THE IMPORTANCE OF IMAGINATION

It all starts with imagination. Albert Einstein once said, "Imagination is more important than knowledge. For knowledge is limited to all we now know and understand, while imagination embraces the entire world and all there ever will be to know and understand."

Of the sixty thousand new students I worked with in my career in higher education, I received exactly one email like the one I described. But if I didn't *imagine* my impact every day and train others to do the same, if I didn't trace my actions and conversations and the potential to change another life's trajectory, what would be the point of it all?

Focusing on those far-reaching effects can transform our lives and work, and enculturating this focus and imagination into an organization and its workforce can transform how it operates.

At the end of this chapter, I'll present an exercise that will help you and those around you adopt a mindset that imagines impact. Thinking systematically starts with understanding your own and your organization's impact on the world.

When we view ourselves as part of a system, we can begin to realize that we can't not matter.

"YOU CAN'T NOT MATTER": SYSTEMS THINKING

People buy into this idea of the ripple effect easily, the proposition that even the smallest act can alter the world. Hollywood has made many successful films that rely on this simple premise—think *Pay It Forward* and *The Butterfly Effect*. We like these clichéd movies about small actions changing the world, but most of us have trouble believing the idea, as evidenced by my children's hospital story. It seems to belong to some drama we'll never be a part of but merely watch from a safe distance.

The space we put between ourselves, our organizations, and the power of our existence and work to alter the world can be dangerous. Remember the Marianne Williamson quote that started this chapter: "Our deepest fear is not that we are inadequate; our deepest fear is that we are powerful beyond measure."

The butterfly effect is a real scientific phenomenon. It occurred in 1969 when Edward Lorenz, a meteorology professor at MIT, was rerunning a weather simulation and forecast for the next two months to confirm its results. This time, however, he mistakenly rounded an input variable from .506127 to .506. Although the adjustment was miniscule, it created chaos and the computer produced a completely different forecast and model for the next two months.[1] The discovery rocked the scientific world and was a foundation for chaos theory, which rests on the assumption that everything in our world has a sensitive dependence on everything else—including people.

Systems are so complex that the smallest change can lead to unpredictable, far-reaching results. The starting premise in systematic thinking is that you and every person in your organization are small parts of the whole we call the world. Everything you do every day changes the world in some way. How do we begin to recognize this impact? How do we empower people who work for and with us to believe they matter, regardless of position? We will explore the answer to these questions in the remainder of the book.

Realizing that you truly matter can change everything, from your level of satisfaction with your job or schooling to your performance to how you make meaning of your existence. When we believe that we matter, responsibility follows, and it's in the act of taking responsibility for our impact on the world that our purpose lies—as individuals and organizations alike.

It's the first step toward awakening purpose.

Unfortunately, we don't get a text message each time we change the world. We won't even live long enough to follow our inevitable impact to its end. That's why it's critical that we daily make our possible impact visible and real to ourselves, the people in our organizations, and the ones we serve. People crave environments that focus on this greater good and benefits are profound.

THE BENEFITS OF A GREATER GOOD MOTIVATION

Research has demonstrated the benefits of greater good motivation in terms of human performance. Wharton School management professor Adam Grant and his colleagues set out to see how a brief interaction between employees and someone their work serves would affect performance. In his landmark 2007 study, Grant and other researchers designed an experimental study and used a group of workers at university call centers. These centers, where workers solicit donations for the school by phone, usually experience high turnover and low morale. In Grant's experiment, the workers in the experimental group had a five-minute interaction with a scholarship student who talked about how the scholarship—funded by the money their calls brought in—had changed his or her life.[2] The control group, another shift at the call center, went on with business as usual.

During the next month, the researchers observed performance. The group of employees who had heard the scholarship student's story had an average per-person donation of more than $500. Before hearing the story, their average had been around $185.

In the study, Grant and his colleagues wrote, "Even minimal brief contact with beneficiaries of our work can enable employees to maintain their motivation."[3] When we believe we matter, and we change people's lives, motivation and results follow.

"MY JOB EXISTS TO SAVE MY OWN LIFE"

I've seen the same effect in my work with a wide variety of organizations. Recently, I was at a Fortune 500 company to work with a group of supply chain and distribution center managers. This group, to be honest, was fairly disengaged. The people seemed worn down by work and didn't want to be there. I was one of the first speakers of the day and could hear people complaining as I walked in.

PRACTICING PURPOSE TIP

Prioritize designing a culture of significance in which all people believe that they and their work deeply matters to the world.

Nothing changed during the session until I asked, *why does your job exist?* A woman toward the back of the room slowly raised her hand and said, "I've been with the company for over seven years, and I just realized last month why I do what I do. I was diagnosed with cancer a month and a half ago, and I realized, lying in the MRI machine, that we supply one of the widgets in it. I realized in that moment that my job existed all this time to help save my own life."

The energy of the room changed. People suddenly began telling their own stories. They became emotionally connected. The rest of the day was positive because in the instant of hearing the story, they weren't just supply chain managers—they saved people's lives.

This is what happens when we focus on how we change the world, when we focus on the human beings' stories at the end of our supply/service chains, and our own lives. Focusing on other people and not on ourselves changes our attitude and our energy. And perhaps most important for organizations and teams, it changes culture.

THE ECONOMICS OF MATTERING:
WE SHAPE HISTORY

An example of how focusing on the greater good can change organizational culture comes from the accounting industry.

KPMG, one of the "Big-Four" accounting firms, was faced with the pressure to differentiate itself in a very competitive industry. After extensive research that included a number of internal focus groups, the company's leadership decided to articulate the firm's higher purpose with the phrase *Inspire Confidence. Empower Change.* Their objective was to help employees and partners to develop a stronger emotional connection to the firm and see their work from a different perspective. In a recent *Harvard Business Review* piece, KPMG's former Vice Chair of Human Resources and Communications, Bruce Pfau, wrote, "We needed to do more than simply announce our purpose and expect it to take hold. We needed employees to experience it for themselves."

The company launched an information campaign around a high-impact video called "We Shape History" that highlighted KPMG's role in significant historic events, such as certifying the election of Nelson Mandela, arranging the lend-lease act that ultimately helped win World War II, and helping with the release of the Iran hostages. The campaign was successful, but KPMG wasn't done. The organization wanted to make its new approach personal, so management asked employees to share their own stories of higher purpose through an app designed to give employees a way to depict the significant difference they make in their work at KPMG.

The goal was ten thousand stories, and employees were promised two paid days off if they reached it. In the end, they submitted more than forty thousand—this from a company with twenty-seven thousand US employees at the time of the campaign. Compelling phrases such as "We champion democracy" and "I help farmers" started being used to describe KPMG's work.

Something powerful had been unleashed. It was as if the potential was always there—with employees just waiting to be asked how their work served a higher purpose.

The campaign benefited the organization in countless ways. When surveyed, more than 90 percent of employees said that the purpose initiative had helped them feel more pride in their work. KPMG's business grew and KPMG rose seventeen spots on Fortune's ranking of the 100 Best Places to Work.[4]

Talk about a competitive advantage! The transformation was all about reflecting on why KPMG did what it did and cultivating people who believed in it at every level. This is the power of leading with authentic purpose.

Why does your company or organization exist in the world? Why should anybody care? There is a human being at the end of every supply chain and every activity on earth, and when we focus on that person, we begin to create a culture of mattering. We begin to awaken our purpose.

FIVE WAYS TO CREATE A CULTURE OF SIGNIFICANCE

Many organizations want to lead with purpose, but few have KPMG's history or resources to draw on. Most don't know where to start. Here are five ways you can begin to create a culture of significance. They are geared toward organizations but can be applied to individuals as well.

1. **Emphasize and reward prosocial values**. Start emphasizing and rewarding prosocial values. Prosocial values put other people and the good of society first. How are such values enacted in your organization? Are they emphasized in your recruitment plan, onboarding and training, performance evaluations, reward structures? People who live out prosocial values show more care for coworkers, deliver better customer service, and are happier.

   The quickest way to topple a culture of meaning is to reward meaningless behaviors, especially self-serving ones. Do you reward self-centered or egocentric behaviors, or do you reward helping and service behaviors? The culture will reflect what you reward. When clients tell me their employees treat each other terribly, I ask, "Do you reward them to do otherwise?" Usually the answer is no, they reward people with commissions, pitting them against each other. It should be no shock that rewarding people who exhibit self-serving behaviors leads to a self-serving culture.

2. **Change the narrative**. When I work with organizations, I sometimes like to sit by the coffee-maker or watercooler and listen. I usually hear complaints about the length of the week or how busy people are or that the weekend is taking forever to arrive. Often, leaders don't realize that what people talk about in the hallways *is* their organization's culture, which in most cases means it's one built on negativity. But positive stories of the impact of the work—like the electronics company worker whose job contributed to her own cancer treatment—are within all of us.

We all have such stories, and we can change the narrative in organizations and in our life to experience the benefits of a greater good motivation. Modeling this kind of inspiring storytelling can be powerful. Start telling these stories in onboarding and training and during performance evaluations.

Use the story of your work's impact to change meetings. Bring customers into weekly or monthly meetings and have them talk about how your product or service changed their lives.

Five minutes of focusing on changing others' lives can make a difference.

For example, in her book, *Selling with Noble Purpose*, Lisa McLeod found that salespeople at firms like Google, Apple, and Procter & Gamble who focused on others and delivered a narrative not centered on results or targets performed better financially over time than those taking a conventional approach.[5] Talk more about others than about results. Do an audit of your processes and procedures and see where you can infuse prosocial values and change the narrative through storytelling.

3. **Do a purpose audit: Why > (How > What).** At talks, I often say that the *why* is greater than the *how*, and the *how* is greater than the *what*. The *why* (purpose) builds more psychological and emotional commitment to an organization or movement than the *how* and the *what* combined. With that in mind, flip the script. You probably train people what to do before they ever become emotionally connected to your *why* or the outcome of your work. Audit how you train people. Consider agendas, evaluations,

BEFORE YOU TEACH PEOPLE WHAT TO DO MAKE SURE TO SHOW THEM WHY IT MATTERS.

etc., and if you're focusing on the *what* first, shift gears to prioritize the *why*. Before you teach people what to do make sure to show them why it matters.

4. **Encourage imagination**. In times of difficulty or burnout, it helps to encourage the imagination of impact. I recently worked on a company's factory floor, trying to engage frontline workers. I found that they were curious about where the product they made went. Of course they were! Create a monthly meeting that highlights the person or cause that your product or service helps—the human at the end of the supply chain. It's an easy way to reframe our impact and encourage imagination. Suddenly workers aren't just putting something in a box; they're saving lives.

5. **Focus on the small.** If you still don't think you matter, consider how you can change another person's brain composition through the smallest of acts.

    For example, in a TED Talk called "The Hidden Power of Smiling," Ron Gutman highlights French neurologists' findings that one smile generates the same level of brain activity as giving someone $25,000 or forty bars of high-quality dark chocolate.[7]

Just by smiling we can literally change the brain composition of a person.

When we believe that we matter and that our work matters, and we bring this reality into our daily lives and organizations, we start to realize we have purpose. We start to awaken it.

It all begins with answering the question: How have you changed the world today?

 ## PRACTICING PURPOSE EXERCISE

This is a powerful exercise for individuals or teams to start learning a purposeful mindset. First, find a quiet five minutes in your day and get out a blank piece of paper, napkin, paper plate, or whatever else you can find to write on. Next, grab something to write with.

1. **Pick an act or task.**

   Think back on your day and choose one self-contained, seemingly insignificant act that you performed. (Hint: pick something you think is routine and boring.) This could be saying hi to another person, smiling at someone, or having a conversation in line for coffee. The key is that you choose an act that happened only once. Try to avoid general actions that span a longer time frame like, "I went to work." Be very specific. Now, write down what you did or said.

2. **Imagine.**

Albert Einstein once said, "Imagination is more important than knowledge. Knowledge is limited. Imagination encircles the world." This is where the fun starts. Start to imagine and follow the "ripple" of the act that you wrote down. Who did and could the act impact? How? Did it change someone's emotions? Did it change someone's mind-set? Someone's perception? Did it change the simple direction they were walking or what flavor latte they ordered?

Now, start thinking about one step removed from your act. What changed as a result of the initial change the act caused? Now keep imagining, step by step, how each act builds on the former, describing what and who changed after each successive act. Keep going until you reach a point of global impact.

Now, if you're like me, you will inevitably get to the point of saying to yourself "no way this would ever happen" or "this is so cheesy." This is the precise barrier you need to break through. Our doubt can consume us and bring us down into a nice, comfortable place called complacency.

3. **Map it.**

As you trace your act, literally draw it out. Draw one arrow or path leading from one effect to the next and write out a short description of each effect as you go. Try to imagine at least ten steps removed from the original act until you reach a global level of impact.

The first time you do this, it will be very hard. But do it daily, weekly, or monthly and it can change your thinking.

4. **Believe it.**

Once you finish your map, you're not done. Now, you have to believe it. Do you believe that this is all possible? What if you did this exercise for every moment in your day?

Imagine if just one of those trajectories turned out the way you imagined. One will. I never imagined that when I said, "Hey, how's it going?" to a fellow student during my summer job it would completely transform her entire life trajectory. But I wish I had every day. My alarm clock would have meant much more.

CHAPTER 5

WHAT'S YOUR PROBLEM?

Success is finding a meaningful need and
filling it better than anyone else.

—*Anonymous*

One of the most powerful ways to awaken personal and organizational purpose is to focus on the human problem you exist (or have the desire) to solve.

PRACTICING PURPOSE TIP

Become clear about what problem in the world you or your organization exists to solve. Separate the solutions you provide from the problem you exist to solve. People care more about the problem.

All of life's endeavors and jobs—and all organizations on the planet—exist to solve some sort of human problem, to fill some human need. And if it's a human problem, it's a *world* problem.

Whether I am working with college students, leaders, or employees, I sometimes get pushback when I introduce the idea of identifying a big "world problem." Some implore that they're not "involved in sustainability or social welfare." Or college students will point out that they haven't finished their degrees or aren't in the kinds of leadership roles that would allow them to address global problems.

Such responses are understandable, but this type of thinking leads us and our organizations into a sense of complacency—turning work, school, and ultimately life into drudgery, leaving purpose dormant.

Remember Mary, the custodian in the first chapter of the book, the woman who came out of retirement to serve as a parent figure on the campus where she'd worked? Like her,

PEOPLE AREN'T EMOTIONALLY MOVED BY SOLUTIONS. THEY'RE MOVED BY HUMAN PROBLEMS.

you might be in a job, educational program, or life situation that doesn't seem world-changing at first glance, but when you activate imagination and focus on the people you serve, every job, every endeavor, every act on this planet becomes important.

Nothing a person or organization undertakes exists for its own sake. Every product we use, company we work for, and academic degree we seek exists to help people and to solve some human problem or to fill a human need or desire.

Identifying that problem is a powerful mechanism for re-centering on and awakening purpose.

We live in a results-obsessed world and operate in an economy and society that profoundly misunderstands what motivates people. We've been conditioned to confuse solutions with problems. The problem you exist to solve is what people care about. It's what engages them. Most likely, it's what engaged you originally, whatever your pursuit, and it's scientifically why stakeholders will commit to your movement or organization.

People aren't emotionally moved by solutions. They're moved by human problems. Your problem is your purpose, and your purpose becomes your story—the narrative of your life and organization.

A recent experience I had with nonprofit organizations highlights this key difference.

CHANGING THE NARRATIVE: PROBLEM VS. SOLUTIONS

At a recent retreat designed to help nonprofits with organizational development, my colleagues and I posed the question to a group of executive directors: *What is the biggest problem facing your organization?*

The first executive director stated, "Money!" There was some nodding and a few sympathetic words, and then the second director said the same thing. As we continued around the circle, eight more executive directors and their board members followed suit, commiserating over money and fundraising issues.

The problem? Money isn't a problem. It's merely one solution that enables you or your organization to solve some important problem. The nonprofits represented that day exist to solve compelling problems, from ensuring that no family goes homeless to ending sexual assault to expanding public access to the arts. They had a long list of diverse and engaging problems but offered a single unengaging narrative: "We need money."

This approach doesn't work in fundraising. No one wants to give you money because you need money. Imagine yourself as a potential donor. You're out to dinner with one of these executive directors, and he or she opens the conversation by saying, "Hey, we really need funds to build a new building."

PRACTICING PURPOSE TIP

Chances are, through what you already do, you are solving a problem or there is an opportunity to identify one. Reflect on what you already do and what problems you already are solving.

It would be easy to talk your way out of donating. *Oh, I'm tied up in other areas right now . . . Tell me the specs of the building again . . . Are you sure you need that much to build it?*

This is what happens when we make solutions our narrative, not only in sales and fundraising but in all aspects of our organizations and lives. People, including you, find a way *out* of committing.

Now, let's imagine you are at that same dinner party and the same executive director says, "Hey I work with an organization that makes sure no child goes homeless; would you consider partnering with us?"

Once the problem is framed in that way, talking your way out of the idea of partnering or donating becomes nearly impossible. You would be have to honestly say to yourself, *You know, today I am not really interested in making sure every child has a home. Can you follow-up next year?*

Focusing on a problem and communicating it internally and externally starts to tell a compelling story that connects with people universally. It identifies the real reason you do what you do, detaching it from solutions and things.

> **WHEN YOU UNITE ALL STAKEHOLDERS AROUND SOLVING THAT PROBLEM, YOUR PURPOSE, PEOPLE BECOME EMOTIONALLY COMMITTED.**

For example, to expand on this hypothetical pitch, a study on why people donate money to nonprofits found 65 percent of people give because they *believe in an organization's cause.*[1] Yet so often, by confusing solutions with problems, the narrative in nonprofits becomes one of scarcity and not opportunity. The same is true with our lives.

And yes, all organizations have causes, including for-profits, because by default, they all solve a human problem. When you unite all stakeholders around solving that problem, your purpose, people become emotionally committed.

Selling widgets is a solution. Getting good grades is a solution. A college degree, revenue, a product, a bridge—

these are all solutions, not the meaningful "world problems" the endeavor existed to solve in the first place.

When we change the narrative in our lives and organizations to find and focus on the human problem we solve, we start cultivating the invisible leader, authentic purpose, and pull people into our movements.

And the problem you exist to solve is the ultimate value-add.

THE FRAGRANCE COMPANY EMPOWERING IMPOVERISHED FARMERS

On its surface, MANE, a fragrance and flavor company that supplies the makers of perfumes and other luxury products, might seem an unlikely world-changer, but that only makes it a more inspiring case of how a global purpose can transform a business.

PRACTICING PURPOSE TIP

Focus on developing empathy and surrounding yourself with empathetic people to identify problems.

I learned about the French firm, which produces flavors and fragrances for everything from beverages to savory foods over the past year, when I connected with Gone Adventurin, a social-impact enterprise founded in Singapore by Laura Allen. Laura's company helps organizations discover global problems they can work to solve through their products, supply chain, organizational operations, and other efforts.

How did Gone Adventurin help MANE identify its problem—and drive profit in the process? Research initiated by the company revealed that 70 percent of worldwide raw materials are produced by smallholder farmers, millions of whom remain impoverished. Poverty among smallholder farmers is one of the most pressing social issues in developing countries, and when such farmers are not empowered, they can't grow enough high-quality raw materials.[2]

With Gone Adventurin's help, MANE took a long look at its supply chain and identified that this was a global problem it could work to solve. In 2015, the company created sustainable-sourcing initiatives in Nepal to develop the market for a new species of pepper called "timur," partnering with grassroots and local nongovernmental organizations (NGOs). Working with other stakeholders, MANE held workshops and trainings that empowered farmers to grow better raw materials and boost their incomes.

The higher purpose was to help remote pepper farmers secure a more sustainable living. Beyond its business goal, however, MANE also immersed its employees in this global problem and used storytelling to involve its stakeholders. The results were transformational. Not only did the project create a market for the timur product and help the economy of Nepal grow, MANE won the first communication prize at the World Perfumery Congress, garnering hundreds of thousands of dollars' worth of free public relations.

A PROBLEM DEVELOPS EMPATHY, WHICH
LEADS TO MEANINGFUL IDEAS

MANE's example shows us just how powerful it can be to reflect on what we do and to identify a big, wicked, global problem. Focusing on a problem develops empathy. Empathy, in turn, often leads to innovation and meaningful ideas.

This was certainly the case for a twenty-nine-year-old named Blake, who was traveling in Argentina in 2006. In a café, he met a woman who was volunteering for a shoe drive. She explained that shoes were a critical issue in Argentina, where many underprivileged kids went without them.

In the days following that conversation, Blake noticed just how many shoeless children there were. He noted the blisters, sores, and infections they suffered. Endless kids, from toddlers on up, it seemed, ran around Argentine streets barefoot. It was dangerous and unhealthy, he thought, as his empathy grew.

PRACTICING PURPOSE TIP

Talk with people you work with or lead regularly about the problem you exist to solve. Create a story behind that problem.

"I wanted to do something about it," he wrote later, "but what *could* I do?"

The answer to that question—which Blake Mycoskie repeated in his 2011 book, *Start Something That Matters*—became TOMS Shoe Company. Empathy interested

Mycoskie in the issue and ultimately led him to develop a social enterprise with a "one-for-one" model. Every time a customer purchased a pair of shoes from TOMS, the company would donate a pair to a child in need.

The concept took off, not necessarily because of the shoes but because of the empathy the story elicited in others, including customers.

Mycoskie saw a powerful example of that empathy when he was checking in for a flight. Rushing from the gym to the airport that day, he forgot to wear his TOMS. He saw a woman wearing a pair, though, and said, "Hey, I like your shoes." She proceeded to passionately relate the story of TOMS. You can imagine her face when she discovered it was him.[3]

Empathy is not only powerful when it comes to identifying a problem and, ultimately, a purpose. It is also contagious, as the TOMS example shows. Dr. Brené Brown said, "Empathy moves us to a place of courage and compassion. Through it, we come to realize that our perspective is not *the* perspective."[4]

We are hardwired for empathy. For example, newborns and infants are said to cry when other newborns cry. We grow up learning to identify problems, whether on the playground or in the classroom, and to help each other address them.

Developing empathy is critical to identifying a problem, which in turn will help clarify your purpose. Here are some proven ways to develop empathy:

- **Surround yourself with empathizers**. We are products of the people around us, so create a community with empathetic people.

- **Become curious**. Curiosity about other people's lives stokes empathy. Instead of "networking" to see how someone can help you, network to learn what problems you can help solve. Passionate curiosity leads to compassionate empathy.

- **Challenge your biases**. Challenge what you think you know about the world and others, and about your organization. Questioning assumptions opens the door to identifying problems and seeing things in a new light.

- **Develop imagination**. As we explored in the previous chapter, imagine the ways you already help to solve a problem in your organization. This is a compelling way to practice thinking about progressively bigger and more complex problems. As MANE did, look at your actions and practices differently, looking for problems you can own and solve. [5, 6]

Once you've worked to develop empathy and, more powerfully, have created a shared sense of empathy in your organization or movement, you and those around you will start to notice more problems. Empathy acts like another sense. It makes us more perceptive to the needs of others, which is why a community or organization of empathizers can be so purposeful.

FINDING A COMPELLING PROBLEM

I recently worked with a group of employees who processed university applications. They had little to no contact with the students applying to or attending the school, and morale was low, according to their supervisors.

> PASSIONATE CURIOSITY LEADS TO COMPASSIONATE EMPATHY.

The job revolved around numbers. Employees' goals related to the numbers of applications they processed in a given amount of time. The numbers of applications received and processed adorned the walls of the workspace, and people continually talked about the work in numeric terms.

PRACTICING PURPOSE TIP

Use existing resources like the United Nations' Sustainable Development Goals to identify and clearly state problems.

I spent a day talking with them and helping them think less about *what* they did and more about *why* they did it. What problem, I asked repeatedly, did they exist to solve?

Toward the end of the day, the group suddenly came to a collective and transformative realization. I referenced a 2012 *New York Times* study, which found just 6.7 percent of the world's population had a college degree. Employees discussed the idea that they *helped to increase the percentage of humans on the planet with college degrees.* Something clicked. They realized this was their problem—one they worked together daily to solve.

At the end of the day, they were fired up. The group came together as a team in ways supervisors hadn't seen in years. Employees were instantly more engaged. They were asking questions. The complaints that had started the day were now framed as barriers to solving this problem of access to a college education.

Being part of a meaningful problem is empowering and awakening. By "problem," I don't mean a small, everyday challenge. A real problem is worth solving and will inspire you and your people forever.

University of California, Berkeley professors Horst Rittel and Melvin Webber call such challenges "wicked problems." A wicked problem is a social or cultural problem that is difficult or impossible to solve for one or more of these four reasons:

1. Knowledge surrounding the issue is incomplete.

2. The number of people and opinions involved are large.

3. The economic burden is massive.

4. The problem is interconnected with other problems.[7]

All meaningful problems worth solving are "wicked." A good place to begin identifying one is by perusing the United

Nations' sustainable development goals or SDGs. They provide a great framework for finding a compelling global purpose and communicating it. The SDGs highlight big, wicked problems, and as you're trying to find yours, either personally or organizationally, they provide the language that can help to identify and articulate it.[8]

These UN goals aim to inspire leaders to think deeper about the big issues plaguing the world, from hunger to gender inequality. The seventeen SDGs offer a shared vision of humanity and a social contract between world leaders and their people. They comprise a to-do list for the planet, a blueprint for success, said Ban Ki-moon, the former UN Secretary General.

HERE ARE THE SEVENTEEN WORLD PROBLEMS INVOLVING SUSTAINABLE DEVELOPMENT THAT THE UN[1] IDENTIFIES:

1. End poverty in all forms everywhere.

2. End hunger.

3. Ensure healthy lives and promote well-being.

4. Ensure inclusive and equitable quality education.

5. Achieve gender equality.

6. Ensure availability and sustainable management of water.

7. Promote sustained, inclusive, sustainable economic growth.

8. Build resilient infrastructure.

9. Reduce inequality.

10. Make cities and human settlements inclusive, safe, resilient, and sustainable.

11. Ensure sustainable consumption and production.

12. Take urgent action to combat climate change and its impact.

13. Conserve and sustainably use the ocean, seas, and marine resources for sustainable development.

14. Protect, restore, and promote sustainable use of ecosystems.

15. Promote peaceful and inclusive societies for sustainable development.

16. Provide access to justice for all and build effective, accountable, and inclusive institutions at all levels

17. Strengthen the means of implementation and revitalize global partnerships for sustainable development.

Here are some additional ways to help you to identify a problem right now.

1. **Consider what bothers you**. Keep a journal for a week, writing down what upsets you about your community. When you drive around town or read the news, what grabs your emotion? What issues do you constantly bring up with friends? What's the one you can't stop thinking about?

2. **Reflect on your personal experiences.** What challenges have you faced that someone might have alleviated? Can you or your organization provide that kind of relief to another? The mark of a true

leader isn't only the ability to look forward, but also to look back and help those who come after you.

3. **Focus on your problem.** Have a retreat or a meeting where you talk only about the human problem you are trying to solve. Ask your team, "What meaningful need in the world are we trying to fill?" This exercise alone may boost commitment. As we explored earlier, research indicates that when people are committed to the greater good, they are happier and perform better.

No matter where you work or live, or what you do, you have a problem to solve. Finding and focusing on it can be a powerful act in awakening a compelling and clear purpose. Clarity is vital if others are to adopt and follow your purpose—an idea we'll explore in the next chapter.

 PRACTICING PURPOSE EXERCISE

1. If you are an organization, hold a meeting with leaders of the organization and reflect on processes, products, sourcing, and other practices. Using the UN SDGs, try to identify a problem that your organization could focus on solving through your practices. Or identify using the language of the SDGs which problem you already exist to solve. How does the problem show up in training and

development, onboarding, performance evaluations, and the overall organizational culture?

OR

2. As an individual, take some time to reflect on what bothers you. Keep a journal for a week and write down what new stories or things in your own community upset you. Now, look back on your week's lists. What themes emerge? What are you drawn to? This could be your "problem."

PART III

CLARIFYING PURPOSE

CHAPTER 6

IDENTIFY AND STATE YOUR AUTHENTIC PURPOSE

Success demands singleness of purpose.

—*Vince Lombardi*

Legend has it that in 1962, President John F. Kennedy visited the space center that would later bear his name to deliver a speech trying to persuade the country that we should invest large sums of money to go to the moon. He bumped into a janitor carrying a broom after mistakenly entering a custodial closet. "What do you do here?" the president asked. Without hesitation, the man replied, "I'm putting a man on the moon."

In the janitor's mind, the purpose of his job wasn't making sure floors were clean; it was getting a man to the moon. That puts a slightly different spin on mopping and sweeping, doesn't it? JFK thought so. It's believed that his famous dictum, "My fellow Americans, ask not what your country can do for you, ask what you can do for your country," arose from such interactions, where a clear, broader purpose beyond self could propel us as a country further than almost anything else. What JFK was talking about was the invisible leader, the common purpose.

The janitor's simple statement—*I'm putting a man on the moon*—is short, memorable, and moving. Who could argue with it? Without workers like him there would be no facility to launch astronauts, but not every custodian takes such a broad view or provides such a clear answer.

PRACTICING PURPOSE TIP

Focus on purpose clarity; it is the most important quality of a powerful purpose.

Stating a purpose as this janitor did—in terms that are clear, emotionally compelling, and easy for a wide variety of stakeholders to understand—is a critical first step in developing purpose clarity.

Starbucks represents one modern example of how to do this effectively. At a recent keynote, I asked the audience if anyone could tell me what Starbucks' purpose is. "What's the mission statement, or what do you think it is?"

A woman in back raised her hand immediately and excitedly. She had just gotten off her shift at—where else?—Starbucks. "Oh, I know what it is," she said. "It's to inspire and nurture the human spirit, one person, one cup, and one neighborhood at a time." She held up her green apron and said, "See, it's right here. We actually have it on our apron, and it's printed in such a way that when we turn it over, we can see it and read it every single day."

Starbucks' purpose is so important, it's on workers' uniforms—not so customers can see it but so the employees can. She went on for almost five minutes about how her Starbucks branch is passionate about this purpose. Managers and workers talk about it every day, and she literally sees it every time she starts work. This purpose is so pervasive that Starbucks trains their employees on how to make human connections before they ever train them on how to make a latte.

The effects of this clear purpose on customers and employees is compelling. Most Starbucks employees have two or three jobs, often working for the coffee chain to make ends meet, but the company's customer-experience ratings are among the highest in the industry. Why? I think it's largely because of that clear, compelling statement that moves people. It's easy to say, I don't want to go to work Monday and make coffee, but it's tough to have a negative attitude about the purpose of "inspiring and nurturing the human spirit." Starbucks' clear purpose makes it almost impossible to remain psychologically disengaged.

When we have a compelling, clear statement that tells us why we exist, it orients, compels, and excites us. We'll spend the rest of this chapter exploring ways to develop and communicate such statements. First, though, a disclaimer: This work is hard. It's not a simple exercise or a statement but a constant, reflective process. Starbucks invests millions in maintaining a purpose-aligned operation.

Having a purpose and awakening it is not enough. Purpose clarity is critical; it is the way in for your stakeholders and anyone else who will join you on this journey.

STATE YOUR PURPOSE CLEARLY

In a 2016 study, Harvard University professor of business administration George Serafeim and New York University professor Claudine Gartenberg devised a way to measure corporate purpose from a sample of 429 US companies. Their metric was based on more than 450,000 survey responses regarding worker perceptions of their employers' purpose.[1]

PRACTICING PURPOSE TIP

Write a clear purpose statement and keep it visible. Share the purpose often and solicit feedback from multiple stakeholder groups. Does it emotionally resonate?

The researchers wanted to find out whether there was a link between financial performance and organizations having a purpose beyond maximizing profit. After analyzing the data, they found no substantial link between having a larger purpose and financial performance.

But that is not the end of the story.

The researchers then analyzed the data a bit more closely, looking at employee responses to certain questions. Organizations where employees responded favorably to statements such as *management makes its expectations clear* or *manage-*

ment has a clear view of where the organization is going and how to get there did outperform organizations lacking a larger purpose.

The researchers called the companies scoring well on such questions "purpose-clarity organizations." Purpose alone is not enough to improve financial results, the authors concluded. The purpose must be clear throughout all levels of the organization. In fact, only those organizations that have high purpose clarity—where leaders and supervisors at all levels know and communicate the purpose clearly—experience better financial results.

The problem is that a lot of purpose work in organizations ends at intellectually knowing there is a larger purpose. We become satisfied with simply saying we exist to solve a world problem. The clarity of that purpose, however, is critical to being a purposeful organization or living a purposeful life. When purpose is clear, we move from knowledge of purpose to *believing* it.

The danger of organizations not clearly stating and consistently reflecting on an authentic purpose, especially at leadership levels, is that they are more likely to make decisions that aren't aligned with why they exist. They also run the risk of copying someone else's purpose or being tempted into what I have called a "default purpose."

The same is true for individuals. I see it every week, teaching college students. It's easy to follow a parent's, advisor's, or instructor's plan for your life—to check off boxes on a curriculum sheet and not have to decide for yourself if decisions are aligned with your purpose. It's easier not to put a stake in the ground and say, "This is why I exist, and this is how I'm delivering it to the world."

College students have become good at following other people's advice—"excellent sheep," as author William Deresiewicz calls them.[2]

When we don't have a clear purpose, we're easily enticed into adopting the purpose of our competitors or our mentors or those who came before us. When that happens, we miss out on what I've described as our most powerful competitive advantage, our authentic purpose.

Stating a clear purpose, writing it down, and sharing it isn't a hollow exercise but a critical part of its fulfillment. Dr. Gail Matthews, a psychology professor at Dominican University in California, found that people are 20 percent more likely to achieve their goals if they write them down and regularly share them with a friend or colleague.[3]

PRACTICING PURPOSE TIP

Connect personal purposes in an organization with the larger organizational purpose to create a common purpose.

When we state something clearly, see and share it regularly, we're psychologically more committed and connected to it in our everyday lives, both as individuals and organizations.

PERSONAL, ORGANIZATIONAL, AND COMMON PURPOSES

Before we move ahead, addressing the key differences and overlap between personal purpose, organizational purpose, and common purpose is important. Creating purpose statements, both individually and for our organizations, is vital. The overlap of those two is "common purpose," and it's a critical component of both organizational success and personal fulfillment.

You can follow the template provided at the end of this chapter with each of these in mind. I recommend continually thinking about personal purpose in all contexts. You can't develop organizational purpose and common purpose without also identifying personal purpose (and empowering the people you lead to do the same).

Personal purpose answers the question, "Why me?" It might address a more local issue, although a personal purpose can be global as well. Why do you, as an individual, exist? Systems-thinking pioneer Peter Senge called working on this question "personal mastery," and it is a critical first step in cultivating the invisible leader, authentic purpose, in life and in organizations.[4]

Personal mastery, Senge states, is sort of a spiritual growth. It cultivates a reason for personal existence that is inextricably tied to one's work. Stating personal purpose clearly and creating a space where everyone in an organization can do so is the starting point for becoming purposeful.

If you lead or are part of an organization, the next question becomes, can every person see his or her own personal purpose in the organization's purpose? If personal purpose answers the question, "Why me?" *organizational purpose* answers the question, "Why this?" It is a statement of the organization's reason for existence, detached from outcomes. Everything I've covered in the book so far should be helping to clarify the answer to this question.

Finally, a *common purpose* answers the question, "Why us?" Why *this* group of people? Why right now? Why are we coming together as individuals to organize, solve this problem, and deliver this purpose? This is perhaps the most overlooked yet most powerful purpose to state. A common purpose answers the questions, *Can every person see his or her own personal purpose in the organizational purpose? Is the purpose shared?*

This is where the real work of cultivating a purposeful organization begins. Answering these questions means having a firm understanding of people's personal purposes. It requires allowing people to state and share them. It requires consciously connecting these personal purposes to the larger organizational purpose. This connection takes intention on behalf of managers and leaders at all levels of the organization. We'll explore how to achieve it in future chapters.

Those not in a position to formally set or develop the purpose of an organization can ask in everything they do: *How does my purpose connect to the larger purpose of the organization?* When the goal the organization is working towards connects with your personal purpose, you become naturally committed to the larger entity. It's a symbiotic relationship: as you deliver your own personal purpose you deliver the organization's purpose too.

Conversely, the organization's delivery of its purpose helps you to deliver yours. This is a powerful idea when it comes to cultivating teams and instilling purpose. But that clear statement of purpose, both in an individual and organizational sense, is critical to starting the process of instilling it.

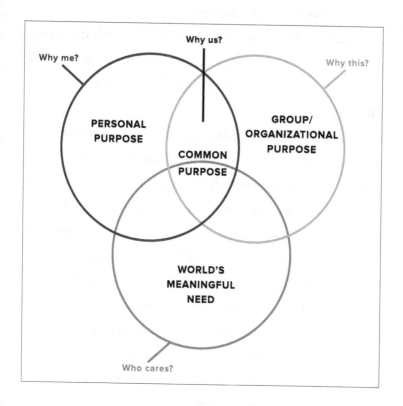

A PURPOSE STATEMENT IS NOT
A MISSION STATEMENT

I want to emphasize here that a purpose statement is not a mission statement. A purpose statement declares why you exist in the world and why people should care. A mission statement declares what you will do. The dictionary defines a "mission" as an assignment or task to be carried out. A purpose is not a task; it is not an assignment or something to be done. *Purpose is the reason for existing.*

Purpose should not be confused with goals or strategy either—a common mistake I'll explore later. When that happens, we lose the psychological benefits of having a purpose.

The odds are good that you have a mission statement or that you've even done a personal vision or mission exercise. Read it now and ask yourself the following questions.

Is your statement worth committing to? This is a key part of an effective personal or organizational purpose. As Simon Sinek writes in *Start With Why*, "We must all answer the question, 'Why do you get out of bed in the morning and why should anybody care?'"[5] Are people really going to work hard to make their employer the best consulting firm in the world or to get a good grade? Maybe in the short term, but such motivation doesn't last. Do you help a friend in need so you can be the best friend in the world?

We all want to contribute to something bigger than ourselves. A powerful purpose taps into people's natural emotional desire to connect with something bigger. Is your purpose statement worth committing to? Is it separated from results and focused on the *why*?

Walt Disney offers us a compelling example of this and quite possibly the most effective start to a purpose statement out there. The start of Disney's statement is, "We exist to create happiness . . ." Later in this chapter, we'll explore why that is such a powerful purpose statement and what differentiates it from a mission statement in the organization's operations.

PRACTICING PURPOSE TIP

Assess your purpose statement using the "components of an effective purpose statement" questions.

Does my purpose statement inspire self-transcendence? Does it inspire you to think beyond yourself and serve others, or does it only help with self-serving goals and outcomes like profit or status? If it doesn't inspire self-transcendence, people probably won't find it motivating or compelling. Again, people want to serve a cause greater than themselves. Research clearly demonstrates, as I noted earlier, that when we're focused on the greater good, we perform better and are more fulfilled.

Is my stated purpose detached from results? Look at your current statement. Are results indicated? Does it mention outcomes, strategies, or goals? Making sure that this statement is detached from results is important.

Is my purpose statement authentic? Is your stated purpose real, original, and genuinely you and your organization, or is it some copy of what other organizations have done? Did you do a mission statement exercise where you modeled yours on another organization's? This is common in modern organizational life, but an effective statement expresses the unique reason why you and you alone exist.

THE ANATOMY OF AN EFFECTIVE PURPOSE STATEMENT

At the end of this chapter, I have included a purpose statement template that you can reflect on as you read the rest of the book. Before we get there, however, I want to go over some of the key elements of an effective purpose statement. These are true for both personal and organizational ones.

PRACTICING PURPOSE TIP

Ensure your purpose is separate from strategies or results.

Stating that *I or we exist* at the start of such a statement is powerful. When you do that, you state, "We (or I) are here, and we are here to solve this problem or fulfill this need." It automatically elicits an emotional connection that tells people why they should care.

The action verb that follows is equally important. What is it you're activating? Think about what *your* action verb is:

to help, to create, to discover, to mobilize . . . What action is inherent in delivering your reason for being? Honing in on the right action verb isn't just a question of word choice. It gets to the core of who you are as an individual or organization and what action you prompt.

The next component is "who." I (or we) exist to do X for . . . *whom?* People are the critical objects of your purpose statement. Realizing this is incredibly valuable because it refocuses the whole organization and you as a person on the fact that you exist to do something *for someone else.* It guides the organization away from being self-serving and toward being self-transcendent.

And finally, what is the outcome or result? What do you want people to think? What do you want people to feel? What do you want people to do because of your existence as a person or organization? For example, using the following template, my example would be: *I exist to help people and organizations awaken and deliver their authentic purpose to the world.* Walt Disney states their purpose this way: *We exist to create happiness . . .*

The popular furniture store Ikea's purpose statement is: *We exist to create a better everyday life for the many people.* As I mentioned, Starbucks' purpose statement reads: *We exist to inspire and nurture the human spirit one person, one cup, and one neighborhood at a time.* Note that focused organizations and strong purpose statements put people at the forefront. They clearly articulate what they want to do for others: to nurture the human spirit, to better everyday life, to make people happy. And these purposes can never be achieved fully, which makes them so inspiring to the people who work for and with them.

Disney structured their stated purpose "to create happiness . . ." in a way that's inclusive, instilling the organization's purpose in every employee. At Disney, whether you clean toilets or are Mickey Mouse, you exist to make people happy. In fact, Disney believes in the idea so strongly that all employees are made *cast members*, with parking attendants just as vital as actors and actresses in creating happiness.

When everybody is committed to a common purpose, it becomes instilled. For example, Disney, before teaching anyone how to do anything, has a class for all new employees called "Common Purpose."[6] The leadership spends time instilling the importance of the invisible leader in all employees to create happiness.

The process is enacted throughout the organization, and the clear purpose of creating happiness becomes a tradition. It becomes a culture. People believe it. This is what our next chapter is about—how to cultivate a life and an organization with a purpose you can state clearly and believe in deeply at all levels.

It is not enough just to know why you exist. It is not enough simply to awaken a reason or to identify a problem. Clearly stating your purpose isn't enough, either. Delivering our purpose is a job for every single day—through every action, process, procedure, and person at every level. It requires inspiring and instilling *belief*.

PRACTICING PURPOSE EXERCISE

Take a moment to fill out this statement template. You can do this as an individual or for your organization. After you have filled it out, share it with people and get feedback. Are they compelled? Do they believe it? Is it authentic? Ask them how it could be more powerful. Do they feel compelled to join you?

Make this statement visible, and we will use it in the rest of the book to work on instilling it in all who interact with you or your organization.

I/We exist to _____(action verb)

_____ (humans, who?) to

_____ (think/feel/do/believe).

Example: I exist to help people and organizations awaken and deliver their authentic purpose to the world.

CHAPTER 7

INSTILL A CLEAR, AUTHENTIC PURPOSE

Belief creates the actual fact.

—*William James*

Stating a clear, authentic purpose is meaningless if you and everyone involved doesn't believe it. Cultivating the belief in an authentic purpose is what makes it real and activates it in our lives and organizations.

And belief is powerful.

In 2004, forty-two-year-old Michael Pauletich noticed a slight shaking in his arm. He began to have trouble smiling and aiming a ball when he played catch with his kids. He saw a doctor and was diagnosed with early-onset Parkinson's disease. In ten years, doctors estimated, he would not be able to move.

He struggled with the disease and the depression that came with it, according to a *National Geographic* article chronicling his story. Then a glimmer of hope appeared. Michael was approved for a clinical gene therapy trial. The procedure involved transplanting healthy genes directly into his brain through two holes doctors drilled into his skull.[1]

It was a harrowing experimental treatment, but it appeared to work. After the surgery, Michael's shaking disappeared and his mobility improved. Perhaps most strikingly, his speech took a turn for the better. Doctors were floored—it appeared the procedure worked miraculously well. Such marked improvements in Parkinson's patients are rare.

Interestingly, when researchers went back and looked at the whole dataset, they declared the trial a failure. There was no statistically significant difference in the reduction of symptoms of those in the experimental group compared to the placebo group. The drug and procedure hadn't worked. But what about Michael?

The researchers went back and looked at the data and found something remarkable. Michael didn't receive the actual drug—he received the placebo. The surgeons hadn't actually operated on his brain, just drilled indents into his head to make him *believe* he had gotten the procedure and was going to get better.

PRACTICING PURPOSE TIP

Make sure your environment (symbols, people, places, things) helps to reinforce your belief in your purpose.

Doctors theorized that the *belief* he was going to get better actually worked better than the expensive gene therapy trial, literally changing the brain's response to his disease.

When we believe something, it becomes our mental architecture of the world and literally changes how our brain responds by producing more dopamine, which is the neurotransmitter responsible for pleasure, behavior, mood, learning, and in Michael's case, movement.[2] Belief physiologically changes us.

Belief, then, is the engine of attitudes and behaviors. When we believe in a bigger authentic purpose, our brains create that reality around us. The philosopher William James said this better than anyone: "Belief creates the actual fact."

The power of belief is one reason why organizations and people who collectively believe in a higher purpose experience more engagement and contentedness; it's a physiological response.

Why am I writing about belief in a chapter about instilling purpose? Because a shared belief is what makes a purpose psychologically beneficial.

WIRED FOR ATTACHMENT

The human brain is wired to find meaning and purpose, and it's also wired for attachment. Dr. Alex Lickerman described this trait in a *Psychology Today* article. "Our brains are attachment machines, attaching not just to people and places but to ideas," Lickerman wrote. Our brains, he argued, become emotionally entangled with the ideas we believe true.[3]

Over time, many psychologists have described religion and other shared belief systems as key unifiers of the human species, helping us to create strong social groups and organizations. This is one reason why religion has thrived and exists in nearly every culture on the planet.

Our beliefs—and not just for the religious—comprise the filter through which we view and react to all experience.

Believing in a purpose orients us. We relate all our activities, actions, and decisions to it. An environment that confirms our beliefs is empowering, and one that denies our beliefs can be devastating. A shared mental architecture that answers the questions *Why are we doing this? Why do we exist?* creates feelings of wellness, drive, and satisfaction within an organization (and our lives). When environments contradict this belief, conflict, dissatisfaction, and cognitive dissonance can ensue.

PRACTICING PURPOSE TIP

Distinguish between knowledge and beliefs. You may "know" a mission statement or purpose statement, but do you believe it in your heart, mind, and soul?

This is why it is critical to create belief by aligning decisions, behaviors, and actions with a larger purpose and designing environments to support and prove it.

KNOWING WHY VERSUS BELIEVING WHY

When I conduct workshops, I usually ask participants to write down in one sentence a belief they have about the world.

From disgruntled employees to new college students to CEOs, nearly everyone who tries this writes down a belief about the world that is compelling and inspirational. Any one of them could be a viral TED talk.

We have become good at knowing why we exist, especially since the popularization of purpose. People frequently do what you did at the end of the last chapter. In organizations, purpose gets plastered on the walls. We include it in the employee orientation binder and the strategic plan we look at every three years, and we hire consultants to help us craft mission statements.

Knowing a purpose, however, constitutes roughly 1 percent of the work in my view. The other 99 percent is *believing* it and instilling that belief in our lives, organizations, and movements. The power of believing in a purpose—mind, body, and soul—is what actually transforms people and organizations.

Consider the NASA janitor from my example in chapter 6. Can you imagine that employee complaining about having to go to work on Monday morning? *Darn. Another week of putting a man on the moon*! It makes no psychological sense.

Now, read the statement you wrote in the last chapter. Does it capture the same sort of imperative and excite you? It should, if it's authentic and tied to a world problem. Do you and the people in your organization truly believe in it? If you do, you won't be able to dread the activity that supports it.

If I believe in my purpose, for instance, it's impossible to say with a straight face, *You know, I'm calling in sick. I just don't feel like inspiring people and organizations to deliver their authentic purpose today.* Likewise, it's hard to picture a Disney employee saying, *Gosh, this creating-happiness job is terrible,* or an Ikea customer wanting to buy from the store across the street that doesn't *exist to create a better life for people.*

The key to these examples, again, is that these companies prove purpose with their practices. Purpose can't just be a statement. It is a way of life that is felt, heard, and seen in everyday personal and organizational life. The decisions we make convey purpose. When we're being purposeful, it permeates our processes, practices, and strategies.

When we structure our environments around purpose, we train our brains to expect that we will make a dramatic difference every day.

DEMOCRATIZING THE SKIES: THE CASE FOR FREE LUGGAGE

Southwest Airlines provides a great example of the power of believing in a purpose. Southwest does not charge for bags and never will. This isn't part of some strategy, but rather reflects the depth of the leadership team's belief in its purpose and the ways they have instilled it throughout the organization.

Southwest Airlines' original purpose was to "democratize the skies," according to founder Herb Kelleher, or more simply put, to provide access to air travel across the socioeconomic spectrum. That purpose came into question when consultants and investors pressured Southwest to start charging for bags, as Roy Spence, the author of *It's Not What You Sell, It's What You Stand For*, recounted in a keynote address. CEO Gary Kelly refused.[4]

Analysts estimated that the company was leaving upward of $300 million on the table, but Kelly wouldn't budge. Reflecting on the airline's original purpose, he believed that charging for bags would most hurt those who could least afford to travel—and violate Southwest's mission.

Kelly told his leadership team to find the money the company was losing on bags elsewhere. Luckily for him, the team also believed in the purpose—so much so that not only did they not charge for bags, they created the very public and well-known "Bags Fly Free" campaign, which drove $1 billion of new revenue and considerable market share to Southwest.

Southwest executives didn't just *know* the purpose of the company, they *believed* it. That belief led them to take a different approach from their competitors and to stay true to their authentic purpose. No other airline was founded to democratize the skies. Their purpose became their competitive advantage, activated by a belief in their reason for existing. Their purpose also served as the impetus of their marketing strategy. Rather than seeking the analysts' views, Southwest dove deep *within*, uncovered its true purpose, and aligned everything with it.

The second lesson we can learn from the example of Southwest is that a belief in purpose resulted in an aligned, albeit difficult, decision under significant pressure. When a group of people all believe in a purpose, the psychological power of the invisible leader in the face of adversity is unleashed.

PRACTICING PURPOSE TIP

Create shared, dramatic experiences for people to get "up close" with your purpose. They need to feel it.

Gary Kelly clearly surrounded himself with people who believed in democratizing the skies. In part four of this book, "Delivering Purpose," I'll provide specific research-backed strategies on how to deliver your purpose and how to design your life and organization to support it, much like Gary Kelly has done with Southwest.

Proving purpose is tough, strategic work. When we just use purpose without putting in the difficult work, we may be at risk of what I call "why-washing," which can be just as destructive to an organization or brand as fraud.

THE FIVE SINS OF *WHY-WASHING*

In the mid-2000s, organizations found sustainability was becoming a key value for both consumers and employees. Following the standard business playbook, they looked for ways to capitalize on it.

Many companies used sustainability solely as a marketing tactic, deceiving people into thinking that their products were sustainable. They used the psychological power of purpose simply to make more money, and to attract more customers and employees. This leap onto the sustainable bandwagon to boost public image has become known as "greenwashing."

In a National Public Radio (NPR) piece about green-washing, the marketing firm TerraChoice evaluated more than a thousand retail products for their environmental claims. Out of that report came the six sins of greenwashing, which ranged from lack of proof to irrelevant claims.[5]

The six major "sins" are instructive in this era of purpose-pedaling and can be translated into what I call "why-washing." Like greenwashing, why-washing is more about image than belief. It lacks substance but uses the power of purpose to create a public perception that you are purposeful.

It is important as you embark on being purpose-oriented to recognize signs you may be why-washing.

THE FIVE SINS OF WHY-WASHING

1. Promoting purposeful branding without purposeful behaviors. This is using a slogan, purpose statement, or imagery to convey a deep understanding of purpose without enacting it for customers or employees.

2. Recruiting for purpose, training for results. Many companies lure college graduates with the promise of a vital purpose and the chance to make a difference, but their training and commission programs solely reward results. This misalignment often produces disengagement, lack of commitment, and high turnover.

3. Letting money trump purpose. If Southwest Airlines had determined that money and profit were more important than its purpose, the company would have started charging for bags in 2010. Difficult situations often determine whether an organization or a person is truly purposeful.

4. Forgetting the front line. Some organizations want to focus only on white-collar purpose. Executives take long retreats to reflect on purpose and go on humanitarian missions. They forget about the front line. How we treat those workers, I believe, is who we are as organizations.

5. Showing no proof of purpose in employees' lives. Authentic purpose engages external stakeholders, but it also is felt through the policies that govern employees' lives. For example, if you say that your accounting firm exists to better people's lives, but you make your entry-level associates work eighty hours a week with no additional pay, you don't exist to better people's lives.

CAUSING NO UNNECESSARY HARM

One example of proving purpose to instill belief comes from Patagonia, the popular purveyor of outdoor clothing and gear. Their stated purpose is to build the best product and cause no unnecessary harm. Patagonia offers ample proof of purpose in its employees' lives and is a model of how to align your reason for existing with daily operations.

An example of this in action was when the company identified overworking the parents of young children as a potential source of harm close to home. Patagonia responded by providing on-site daycare and nurseries at no extra cost, as part of employees' compensation.

Three decades later, 100 percent of female Patagonia workers who had children during the previous five years returned to work. The company has a 100 percent retention rate for new mothers, significantly higher than the US average of 79 percent.[6]

Interestingly, about 50 percent of managers and senior leaders at Patagonia are women. They know that to deliver their purpose they have to prove it on the front line, to do no harm to families and kids because of their work, and to build the best product. They are making sure they retain their most talented women, who are some of the most influential leaders of the organization.

HOW TO INSTILL PURPOSE

How do you go about instilling and aligning purpose?

Make your purpose known and clear, starting with every manager and supervisor. We tend to think of managers as the ones who hire, fire, plan, and buy. I think we should redefine management and leadership as the group of people responsible for over 40 percent of the waking lives of human beings. Making sure that the managers and supervisors bearing that responsibility are clear about an organization's purpose shows through their management style.

Tell the story of why you exist, often. Talk about *why* before *what* in meetings. Reward *why* before *what,* and train people by first engaging them in your story.

Create shared dramatic experiences. People need to feel your purpose. How do your people know when organizational purpose has been delivered? How do they hear about it? Do they see it? Do they feel it? More important, do they experience it together?

A direct example of how your service or product truly changes or enhances a human being's life is a reinforcing feedback loop that authentically motivates your people. It also helps to create an environment that confirms belief in the purpose.

Create the spaces for dynamic storytelling by bringing people whose lives you have improved in to speak to your team. This can go a long way toward creating a sense of unity and instilling a higher purpose.

Research on successful organizations, especially non-profits with cultures of service above self, reveals a common theme of employees having some sort of shared experience delivering the mission together. They experience an event, a news story, a blog, or a photograph that inspires them to act and to join the cause. Every organization has such stories. Tell them often.

Design people's first experiences on purpose. First experiences with an organization are a vital, though often overlooked, component of instilling purpose. The first experiences we have with an idea, organization, or movement stay with us, so make sure that your employee on-boarding and any and all stakeholder experiences begin with the story of *why*.

Focus on engagement of all your stakeholders on purpose. Cultivating a belief in *why* you do what you do before exploring *what* you do is critical for every stakeholder group. You can do this both personally and organizationally. As people, we have stakeholders in our lives: our friends, family, colleagues, advisors. All these people know why we do what we do. How do we enroll them in our stories to support us as we move along this journey? Author Paul Ratoff, in his book, *Thriving in a Stakeholder World: Purpose as the New Competitive Advantage*, calls this your "stakeholder world." Identifying your key stakeholders and enrolling them in your purpose is critical.

Surround yourself with the right people. Make sure that you partner with or hire people who believe what you believe and aren't just good at what they do.

PRACTICING PURPOSE TIP

While the people you surround yourself with surely don't have to agree with you, they should believe in your purpose.

There's an old story of Southwest Airlines bringing in pilots for group interviews and asking candidates to try on the Bermuda shorts that were part of Southwest's summer uniform. The pilot interviewees who didn't want to wear shorts were led into a different room and quickly told they were not a good fit for Southwest.

The company's mission—and the culture, attitudes, and beliefs supporting it—was so important that management didn't even consider the qualifications of the eliminated pilots. The first cut had everything to do with *why;* the *what* came later.

This brings us to the last part of the journey and the key to purposeful living, leadership, and organizational design: proving it on a daily basis.

After all, no one cares why you do what you do unless you prove it every single day.

 PRACTICING PURPOSE EXERCISE

Think back to a cause or movement you cared about and believed in. Now, try and dissect it. What made you believe in the purpose? What behaviors of the leaders made you buy in? What made this movement different?

How can you replicate these experiences in building your own movement or organization?

PART IV

DELIVERING PURPOSE

CHAPTER 8

THE INTEGRITY OF PURPOSE

You are what you do, not what you say you'll do.

—Carl Jung

Banking giant Wells Fargo clearly made purpose alignment a stated priority in the preamble to its vision and values statement: "We believe in values lived, not phrases memorized. If you want to learn how strong a company's ethics are, don't listen to what their people say. Watch what they do."[1]

The key words in the statement are "we believe." As we've seen, belief actualized can be incredibly powerful. If Wells Fargo truly believed its statement, its ethics should be clear. After all, the bank essentially restated Carl Jung as quoted above: "You are what you do, not what you say you'll do."

Taken at its word, the idea is inspiring. Even more inspiring was the "Culture of Caring" mantra that Wells Fargo believed in firmly enough to trademark. On its website, the company explained what these words meant, promising to be warm, welcoming, and humble and to have the empathy to make a difference in people's lives. This mindset was supposed to permeate every level of the organization and every tier of employees.[2]

But in mid-2016, some of the bank's customers noticed they were paying fees on accounts they'd never opened. A consulting group was quickly hired to investigate. What it found was shocking; more than 5,300 of the bank's employees had secretly opened more than 1.5 million deposit accounts, which incurred fees the customers never authorized.

The consulting firm described the practice as widespread and said that frontline employees, who made around $12 an hour, had opened most of the fraudulent accounts. The bank was fined $185 million by the US Consumer Financial Protection Bureau—the largest fine in the bureau's five-year history.

So how did the goals of a "Culture of Caring" and ethics demonstrated by actions not words result in behaviors so badly misaligned with the stated purpose?

The lessons learned from studying this case are key to understanding why—as Simon Sinek in *Start With Why* put it—"the *why* goes fuzzy."

Such fuzziness was evident in Wells Fargo's reaction to the scandal, which, like many responses to fraud, blamed the problem on a small percentage of employees. This might have been true, but it missed the point. Alignment of purpose takes a systemic, cultural effort. Ethics and values are a system created in our lives and organizations. The numbers of employees

"INTEGRITY OF PURPOSE" IS CONSISTENCY OF AND ADHERENCE TO OUR PURPOSE.

involved, their wages, and titles don't get to the heart of the problem.

The bank's purpose misalignment had deeper roots, though the ways the organization slipped are all too common.

PURPOSE MISALIGNMENT: DEFINING THE TERMS

Before continuing to use terms like "ethics" and "integrity," it is important to define them.

- **Values** are principles we use to define what is right, good, and just. They are the fundamental beliefs we hold about the world and proper conduct.

- **Morals** are the values we attribute to a system of beliefs, such as a political party, culture, religion, or organization.

- **Ethics** are a code of moral principles that guide a person's or group's behavior. Ethics are values-enacted—where the action is.

- **Integrity** is the consistency of adherence to your values, morals, and ethics. It means you consistently are making decisions that align.

Expanding on the general definition of integrity, "integrity of purpose" is consistency of and adherence to our purpose. We achieve it through our values, morals, and ultimately, through the ethics guiding our behavior. When they are aligned in everything we do, we have integrity of purpose.

PRACTICING PURPOSE TIP

Look for the four symptoms of purpose misalignment in your life or organization.

Recognizing the symptoms of purpose misalignment in an organization or in our own lives is critical for upholding integrity of purpose. Here are the four symptoms of purpose misalignment:

FOUR SYMPTOMS OF PURPOSE MISALIGNMENT

1. **Focusing on results**. The Wells Fargo situation exemplifies what happens when we focus on results or things for motivation.

   The bank's unethical sales practices were driven by two major things: a leadership obsession with quotas, which were incentivized, and a culture that prioritized these results over people—employees and customers. The thing we reward becomes our culture. If, for example, you state that you have a culture of caring but reward self-serving behaviors, you're already out of alignment.

   The same misalignment can happen to us as individuals. If we say we exist, for example, "to be there for others" but reward ourselves with free time by not calling back a friend in need, our purpose is not delivered.

But when we train our minds and our teams to focus on others and the greater good, short-term, results-based incentives have a tougher time taking over. If the culture of Wells Fargo had focused on the well-being and lives of the people it served, building rewards around that purpose, the institution may not have faced the disastrous misalignment that occurred.

2. **"Goals gone wild**." In a 2009 paper entitled "Goals Gone Wild: The Systemic Side Effect of Overprescribing Goal Setting," University of Arizona Management Professor Lisa Ordonez and colleagues found that goal setting actually has adverse effects when we focus on the goals obsessively.[3]

    Her research included two major findings: goals cannot create self-sustaining motivation and goals can't be the only focus of leaders.

    Goals only work in the short term. A goal or a result can increase extrinsic motivation or motivation toward something outside a person (a task) but decrease intrinsic motivation—the internal reward you feel by accomplishing something for its own sake.

When we attach tasks to some "thing" to be achieved, what happens after we achieve it? It's on to the next thing. We're never satisfied. Such goals are too narrow. They don't allow a larger perspective. The lack of a broader view can drive us into isolation, since we don't have to recognize any impact beyond ourselves and the immediate task or decision.

Many goals also have unrealistic time horizons. We pressure ourselves to complete a task too quickly, which opens the door to cheating as a way out. This occurred in the Wells Fargo case, where compensation was tied directly to achieving goals rapidly.

Goals that are too narrow, difficult, or pressing open the door to unethical behavior. People begin to rationalize ethically questionable behavior for the sake of the goal. Fear of failure and dissatisfaction aggravate what can become desperate measures as we lose sight of the people we set out to serve. Purpose pulls us out of this isolation and returns accountability.

3. **Getting caught up in the moment**. Research shows that unethical behavior doesn't necessarily reflect your personal values. Humans are situational and reactionary, and the particulars of a situation, from declining sales to personal troubles, can influence our decisions.[4]

Many of the employees who opened fake accounts at Wells Fargo were, no doubt, honest people overall. If, however, your job supported your family and earning enough to provide for them seemed contingent on opening fake accounts to meet unrealistic goals, you can see how environmental pressures might elicit unethical behavior.

Awareness of the environmental pressures that impact our decision making and ethics is important. Reflect on your purpose and make the space to consider alternatives before you decide. Creating such space in personal and organizational life allows us to step back and reflect on alignment with our "why."

4. **Normalizing unethical behavior.** In the early 1990s, a key study by psychologists Robert Cialdini, Raymond Reno, and Carl Kallgren found we are more likely to litter in a park if we see others litter. We define "normal" by what others do, which means unethical behavior and purpose misalignment may be contagious. Seeing others abandon purpose makes it acceptable for you to abandon purpose too.

Focusing on the people you surround yourself with and the norms you establish to achieve purpose alignment is critical. I often see this phenomenon with college students, whose purposes range from becoming doctors to teachers to journalists. Whatever their aim, when they see peers—especially friends—skip class, they begin to skip class too.

The good news is that if unethical behavior is contagious, so is ethical and purposeful behavior. Organizations can encourage behaviors oriented toward the greater good and a belief that the work matters. In our lives and organizations, purpose can be contagious.

HOW TO ALIGN PURPOSE

I keep this anonymous quote at the front of everything I do: *You are your last worst decision.* Forcing yourself to reflect on every decision and the alternatives is a good first step toward purpose alignment.

Create the space to assess and reassess. Try to assess everything involved in a situation before you make a decision. Professor Robert Nash, who specializes in applied ethics at the University of Vermont, provided a useful guide to ethical decision making that helps us understand a situation in its totality.[5] Nash offers a framework of pointed questions people should ask themselves before making a decision. His process forces people to make the kind of necessary space I have been

> THE GOOD NEWS IS THAT IF UNETHICAL BEHAVIOR IS CONTAGIOUS, SO IS ETHICAL AND PURPOSEFUL BEHAVIOR.

talking about—the time and room to consider all pertinent factors and alternative choices.

The following seven questions draw on Nash's work, as

PRACTICING PURPOSE TIP

Create space between when you experience external pressure and when you make an ethical decision.

---

well as our explorations of purpose in earlier chapters. They form a framework that will allow you to take stock of your decisions and purpose alignment when facing an ethical dilemma. They apply equally to individuals and organizations of all kinds, so the "you" in each can refer to either a person or an organization, depending on your context.

KEY QUESTIONS FOR PURPOSE ALIGNMENT

Ask these questions of yourself or your organization when purpose is at stake in a critical decision:

1. What are the moral issues, and how do they fit with my purpose? Every purpose statement is a statement of values. Once you state your purpose, you're saying you value this stated *why*. How does that purpose inform the moral issues?

2. What is your initial intuition? Sometimes our gut reactions are the most important pathways to purposeful behavior. What did you initially think

you should do? What will help you sleep better at night?

3.   What ethical conflicts arise when you start making the decision? What conflicts arise internally as you move toward determining what you'll do, how you'll structure the organization, or how you'll respond to someone? Think about those, and write them down.

4.   Who are the major stakeholders? Write down every stakeholder group that could be affected by this decision. Often, this simple exercise reminds us there are multiple people dependent on the delivery of our purpose.

5.   What are the foreseeable consequences? If I or we were following my purpose, what would be the ideal consequence? Follow every option to its end. How would your purpose be delivered or not delivered in each scenario?

6.   How do your beliefs about the way the world should be guide your thinking about this situation? Interrogate yourself about your beliefs. How should people behave? Are you acting in accordance with what you believe?

7.   If you were acting in your ideal character, the person that you most want to be, what would you do? Can you live with your decision?

Asking these seven questions as you reflect on purpose alignment is a great exercise for individuals as well as for leadership groups and teams.

Put purpose at the center of your decision-making processes. Make sure everybody in your organization or your life understands how purpose-aligned decisions are made

---

PRACTICING PURPOSE TIP

Create goals that are not too narrow, are not unrealistic, and are tied directly to your purpose and not results.

---

when faced with ethical dilemmas. Normalizing decision-making processes in an organization can help ensure purpose alignment. Create a "decision tree" that shows on paper (or a screen) how decisions are made in your organization. Just mapping the decision-making process will help you find areas where you're susceptible to purpose misalignment.

A solid decision-making process won't eliminate all uncertainty, however. Ask other like-minded people before you act. What would they do? Seek advice from people outside your organization. Use contacts with your competitors to consider what they would do. Ethics and purpose-alignment are community efforts. We need exposure to a system of thinking and a variety of outside perspectives to nudge us out of the isolation that focusing on an outcome creates.

Talking to others can foster creativity, which is vital. Dilemmas can become opportunities for growth, as we saw with the example of Southwest Airlines turning a financial loss on baggage charges into its successful "Bags Fly Free" marketing campaign.

What are your alternate ways forward? If you feel trapped into doing something not aligned with your purpose, ask yourself, "What if this wasn't so? What are all the alternative courses of action, and what would happen if we followed each of those?"

If a colleague or your organization as a whole seems to have fallen into one of those traps and is behaving in a way

---

PRACTICING PURPOSE TIP

Create a process that allows you to "check" yourself before making decisions.

---

not aligned with an espoused purpose, speak up. Simply asking questions about a process can highlight the places we can change and the ways misalignment has occurred.

Ultimately, what you risk reveals what you value. What are you willing to give up? If you risk results to uphold a belief in your purpose, you are probably in alignment. If there's a habit of decision making like Southwest's, you're on the right track. But if you consistently risk purpose for results (profit, quotas, grades, a degree), you're not purpose-aligned.

Do you put your money where your purpose is? If you were a huge outdoor retailer, would you give up tens of millions in Black Friday earnings for your purpose? Patagonia did just that. Patagonia's mission, as we explored earlier, is to do no harm and to create the best products with as little environmental impact as possible. With that purpose of environmental stewardship in mind, Patagonia donated its $10 million of revenue on Black Friday to environmental groups—showing through behavior that it cares about the environment. What the organization risked revealed what it values.

REI, the big outdoor retailer, closed its doors completely on Black Friday and instead paid its employees to

> STATING A PURPOSE EXCITEDLY IS GREAT, BUT IF WE DON'T GET EXCITED ABOUT UPHOLDING IT THROUGH THE BEHAVIOR AND TOUGH DECISIONS WE ENGAGE IN EVERY DAY, IT WILL FADE.

"opt outside." REI's purpose? "Inspiring, educating, and outfitting its members and the community for a lifetime of outdoor adventure and stewardship." Rejecting the overwhelming consumerism of the biggest shopping day of the year in favor of outdoor adventure aligned perfectly with this organization's purpose. But the gesture wasn't easy. Not only did REI forgo the immense revenue of Black Friday sales, the company also bore the expense of paying all its employees to take the day off and go outside.

To adopt the invisible leader and build a purposeful life or organization requires aligning our values, ethics, and actions with our purpose. Stating a purpose excitedly is great, but if we don't get excited about upholding it through the behavior and tough decisions we engage in every day, it will fade.

As Carl Jung's quote at the start of this chapter asserts, "You are what you do, not what you say you'll do." In the

---

PRACTICING PURPOSE TIP

Think creatively when responding to situational pressures. How can you act and be in alignment with your purpose?

---

remaining chapters, we'll focus on actions and tangible strategies you can enact to further deliver your purpose in your life and organization.

 # PRACTICING PURPOSE EXERCISE

Think about an ethical dilemma you are facing in your life or your organization. Now, use the seven questions provided in this chapter to analyze the situation. How does this process change your thinking?

CHAPTER 9

DESIGNING A PURPOSEFUL ORGANIZATIONAL CULTURE

Work is about a search for daily meaning as well as daily bread, for recognition as well as cash, for astonishment rather than torpor; in short, for a sort of life rather than a Monday through Friday sort of dying.

—*Studs Terkel*

I was recently invited to give a talk to a group of bus drivers at a local school district. The client who invited me asked me to inspire and motivate the employees, but politely warned they might not be the most engaged audience. First, the client told me, the training was required, and second, supervisors had received negative feedback from the group after previous workshops on leadership and personal development.

For many of the bus drivers and mechanics, this was a job to pay the bills, and many faced financial difficulties. Understandably, supervisors thought purpose was not on these employees' radar. This characterization reflects the most common objection I hear when it comes to my work and research. "Well, Zach, how can people find purpose when they are struggling to find a paycheck?" or "They're just here for the money."

This kind of attitude creates a self-fulfilling prophecy. When we make pay or other physical resources the magic bullet for solving turnover and engagement issues, we focus on scarcity and leaders who treat people as if they don't want meaning can never elicit it.

Contrary to what I heard from the school district supervisors before my talk, I quickly learned that those bus drivers already *were* inspired and motivated—at a level far deeper than I could have imagined. They simply needed to be asked the right questions and given the right environment to elicit the meaning in their lives and jobs.

PRACTICING PURPOSE TIP

Build in regular, consistent, and authentic gratitude and affirmation.

During my talk, I asked the bus drivers to write a short account of one time when they felt their job mattered in the world. As I transcribed their handwritten notes, this quote was one of the first:

I felt like my job mattered when I went to a funeral of a young student. He went to school (pre-K) every day with many physical problems and a do-not-resuscitate tag on his wheelchair. One day, we went to pick him up from school, and his dad came out and told us his son was dying. At the funeral, I was impressed that a four-year-old had drawn hundreds of mourners. His parents told me that his son's ride to school was the highlight of his short life.

Another driver wrote: *I felt like my job mattered when a student who had MS said, "I wish people wouldn't make fun of me." I said, "Everyone is different for a reason. You are an amazing person." Then he smiled.*

And another highlighted his role as a listener: *I felt like my job mattered when I could listen to upset students, let them vent and calm down . . . when students feel happy and safe on the bus because they trust me.*

The supposedly "tough crowd" of bus drivers wrote more than seventy accounts like these. All displayed similar levels of emotion, and the same awareness of deep meaning in their work. How had the leadership team missed this facet of its employees?

As is often the case in organizations, these stories of impact and meaning had been locked away, weighed down by regulations, mandatory training, and the broad stereotypes we all have about what motivates us. "They just need a paycheck . . . They just want their benefits . . . It's just a job."

As you read these excerpts, you might have felt these bus drivers were not really bus drivers so much as counselors, mentors, and teachers to students. The experience again reminded me that it's not about what we do, but why we do it. Leaders who cultivate the invisible leader of authentic purpose can design organizational cultures that unlock such meaning and potential.

Reading the bus drivers' stories, I noticed common themes. The drivers felt like they mattered when they experienced four major things:

1. **Gratitude and affirmation, a feeling of significance**. Nearly every story included a source of gratitude and affirmation regarding the job the bus drivers did, and it was always the most significant contributor to their feeling that they mattered. Often the gratitude came from the children or their parents, but supervisors who shared such stories and thanks secondhand with employees were also significant.

2. **A focus on making a difference**. When bus drivers focused on and could articulate the differences they made in the lives of students or parents, they tended to feel as if their job mattered more.

3. **A greater responsibility**. In numerous bus driver narratives, employees felt personal significance when told that apart from providing transportation, they were teacher or parent figures, or they kept kids safe.

4. **Difficult challenges**. Employees seemed energized and felt like they mattered most when they were able to overcome a significant challenge, such as transporting difficult children or problem solving in the moment.

Those who lead with authentic purpose can unlock these stories of mattering and create environments where people feel significant—where they see that their jobs benefit not just their bank accounts, but the totality of their lives, making them better people overall. This kind of meaning doesn't just happen, however. It must be designed as consciously as we design financial statements or any other vital process in our organizations.

WHY MEANINGFUL WORK?

Why elicit this sense of meaning at work? Over the course of their lives, people spend almost 40 percent of their waking time at work. This is where they engage in what oral historian Studs Terkel called "a daily search for meaning" in *Working*, a landmark project based on extensive interviews with employees in a wide variety of occupations.[1]

> **THE PRIMARY ROLE OF MANAGERS, SUPERVISORS, AND LEADERS OF ALL KINDS IS TO BE RESPONSIBLE FOR 40 PERCENT OF PEOPLE'S LIVES.**

The primary role of managers, supervisors, and leaders of all kinds is to be responsible for 40 percent of people's lives. If those lives are to be meaningful, work must be meaningful. We are wired to search for meaning, so designing environments that foster meaning in organizations is more than just a good idea for modern leaders. I argue it's a moral responsibility and the most important skill leaders can have.

After awakening and clarifying purpose, designing environments that elicit the experience of meaningful work is critical. Psychologists Michael Steger, Bryan Dik, and Ryan Duffy set out to design and validate one of the first comprehensive instruments to measure meaningful work. They called it the Work and Meaning Inventory (WAMI). They found that people consider their work meaningful when they experience three major things:[2]

1. They feel like they are significant and that they matter.

2. They have a "greater good motivation," or a focus on people beyond themselves.

3. They feel like better all-around people because of their jobs.

MATTERING: BUILDING AN ENVIRONMENT OF SIGNIFICANCE

We're going to explore strategies for enacting each of these components, but first I want to emphasize that reflection is critical to designing meaningful work. Thinking honestly and deeply about your organization's current environment and culture is the first step in fostering *mattering* over *marginality*. I'm borrowing those terms from scholar Nancy Schlossberg, who is often quoted in student-development literature in higher education.[3] Understanding this dichotomy is key to designing a purposeful organizational culture.

Think about a time when you felt marginalized. What were the words that made you feel this way? What were the actions? What was the environment like? How would you describe feeling marginalized? Now, think about a time when you felt like you truly mattered. What were the words that made you feel that way? What were the actions? What was the environment like? Reflecting on personal experiences of mattering and marginality is a powerful path to understanding how, as leaders, we can make sure others feel like they matter.

People are more likely to feel they matter when we create what Dik, Duffy, and Steger called "an environment of significance." One of the most powerful strategies to build such an environment sounds simple but is often overlooked: gratitude. Simply expressing consistent, meaningful, personalized gratitude is vital.

PRACTICING PURPOSE TIP

Reflect on key moments in your life and work when you felt like you mattered. Replicate that experience for others through both personal and organizational actions.

The second way to build an environment of mattering, as I noted in the bus driver example, is to provide steady affirmation. This is not just for the year-end awards banquet but should be woven into the fabric of the culture. Workers need to be affirmed for being there, delivering your organization's important purpose.

HOW TO GIVE INSPIRING AFFIRMATION

One model of affirmation that is especially useful is by the author of *Feedback That Works,* Sloan Weitzel. The "SBI" model focuses on situation, behavior, and impact.[4] Following this template when you give feedback helps people emotionally commit to your purpose and feel like they matter.

Here's how it works. First, when you give affirmation, be clear about the situation or context. For example, "Yesterday, halfway through the 9:00 a.m. meeting when everyone's energy seemed low for Zach's presentation, you perked up and . . ." Identifying the moment with that level of specificity is powerful.

PRACTICING PURPOSE TIP

Treat yourself and others as they **can** *be.*

Second, identify the behavior, describing what people did in the situation. "Yesterday at 9:00 a.m., when Gary presented his plan, you were smiling and engaged and nodded in a way that seemed to give him confidence . . ." Noting the specifics of the behavior—smiling, comments, body language, etc.—gives the affirmation weight. If I were praising bus drivers from the earlier story, for example, I might focus on how they looked or what they said when they welcomed a student.

Finally, what was the impact? Praising people's behavior is great, but saying how their words or actions made others *feel* amplifies the effect.

When we offer affirmation in this way—noting the situation, behavior, and impact—people appreciate exactly where, when, and how their actions mattered. They're more likely to continue the behavior because they've not only been recognized for it, they also can identify exactly what they did and its positive impact.

Making sure that all supervisors and leaders are trained on how to give specific affirmation is a good way to start building an organizational culture that fosters purpose and meaning.

INSTILLING A GREATER GOOD MOTIVATION

The second set of strategies focus on making a difference and cultivating a greater good motivation. In chapter 4, I described the powerful effect of one woman who was part of a Fortune 500 electronic company's supply chain management team. When she announced that their company made one of the widgets in the MRI scanner used in diagnosing her cancer, her job, she realized, existed to help save her own life.

Her highlighting that greater good inspired her fellow supply chain managers, but in working with the company, I realized that workers on the distribution center floor had no idea where the widgets they were shipping went. They were curious, but no one thought they wanted to know some went into military aircraft and some into medical equipment—that all were a part of some compelling human story.

The company is working toward highlighting where its widgets go and discussing the people and organizations they help. When we show people why the work matters, it inspires a greater good motivation.

PRACTICING PURPOSE TIP

Invest in the whole person. Make sure that what they do makes their whole lives better.

Think about the potential impact of this company's simple change on its workers' self-concept. They will be able to go home and say, "Hey, I was part of the process that made a medical device work for someone or helped an aircraft fly." Such simple storytelling—changing the narrative and shifting the focus in weekly meetings from the *what* to the *why*—creates greater good motivation. Having customers or various stakeholders come in regularly to tell their stories about your product or service, as I suggested in chapter 7, has a massive impact on greater good motivations.

The third aspect of Steger, Dik, and Duffy's model of meaningful work was that the work must be seen as benefitting someone's whole life. The assumption underlying this idea is that *every person has high potential and goals.* When people see their environment as helping to achieve their visions, they naturally become more loyal. There is a surge of practical models to help companies identify and develop "high-potential" employees. I argue that everyone should be viewed as high potential.

The philosopher and writer Goethe said, "If you treat an individual as he is, he will remain how he is. But if you treat him as if he were what he ought to be and could be, he will become what he ought to be and could be."

When we treat the people in our organizations as the ideal vision of themselves, they often become it. This is why investment in personal development is critical.

For example, before anybody starts at your organization, you could ask, "What is your vision for your life? What do you want out of life, and how can our organization help you get there?" Connecting people's personal purposes to the organization's purpose creates that vital sense of common purpose.

Common values are key too. It's helpful to focus your processes, from recruitment to hiring to onboarding, on aligning personal and organizational values. Accomplishing this requires understanding what your people value. In one-on-

EVERYONE SHOULD BE VIEWED AS HIGH POTENTIAL.

one meetings, you can ask questions like, "What are the top values in your life?" How do the organization's values align with the answers? How do you find the right fit for that employee to enact his or her values? When people see themselves in your vision, it becomes a reality for them.

In addition, research finds that fostering community and social-networking opportunities allows work to benefit a person's entire life.[5] When people feel like they are a part of something bigger than themselves at work, when they feel like they have a sense of community, they're healthier and happier—both in and out of work. Social networking often comes in the form of informal interactions. Designing a workplace that encourages people to eat lunch together, maintain relationships, and tell stories, is beneficial in innumerable ways. More importantly, it gives people the feeling that they are a part of something significant.

MEANINGFUL WORK INSPIRES EMOTIONAL COMMITTMENT

Meaningful work inspires one of the most powerful aspects of any organization: emotional commitment. Emotional commitment is defined as the emotional attachment to an organization as manifested by an individual's identification with and involvement within that organization. As part of a paper I published in the *Human Resource Development Review*,[6] I looked at more than seventy-five years of research on the types of commitment that motivate people. The result of that research is clear: emotional commitment has the most powerful impact on positive organizational outcomes like low turnover and engagement.

Let's do a quick thought experiment. Pick someone in your life who you love. Now, write down the reasons why you love that person. People often write down that the person they love helps them feel good about themselves, they are loyal, and they help them when they need it

The things you wrote down are the key factors in building a culture of purpose that fosters emotional commitment. Committed employees want to remain in the organization. They care for the organization because the organization cares for them. They're willing to give a strong effort for the organization and have a deep belief in its values.

In the psychological literature, this type of commitment is called "affective commitment." Nearly all the research shows that it is the only type of commitment that has a steady correlation to lower turnover, higher organizational performance, and deeper engagement. Ironically, modern organizations, including nonprofits, seem to invest in this type of commitment least of all.

Asking the following questions can be revealing of your organizational culture:

- How much time do you focus on cultivating the connections between your people and the purpose of the organization?

- How much time and money is spent on interviewing and onboarding that focuses on inspiring a love for the organization and its purpose?

- How much training and development money is invested in developing an emotional bond between the individual and the organization?

- Does your organization look immediately to "what" solutions, like salaries, to maintain engagement and commitment?

The answers to these questions have big implications.

KEY AREAS TO FOCUS ON

Here are some key areas to focus on in designing an organizational culture that elicits purpose and meaning to inspire emotional commitment:

- **Socialization.** This starts with people's first experience of your organization. Researchers have found that when employees don't feel positively connected to the values and mission of the organization in their first two weeks, they're twice as likely to leave within the first year.[7] Onboarding should focus on building values, congruence, and pride in the purpose of the organization. It should foster feelings of care for the organization.

- **Trust.** Bottom-up trust-building achieves emotional commitment better than top-down efforts. Those direct supervisor-supervisee relationships are critical. What does trust mean to your organization? What does trust mean to those responsible for people in your organization? Trust is often built in quiet, nonvisible ways. Focusing what is "heard in the hallways," is critical. What do people talk about before and after meetings, when they're walking to the parking lot? Is it griping and gossip or positive narratives?

- **Mentoring**. Do you have structured mentoring relationships centered on how to deliver the organization's purpose? Mentoring relationships have an incredibly positive effect on levels of emotional commitment. The mentor, however, must be emotionally committed to the organization. Who does the mentoring is as important as having mentoring. I often see organizations with "mentorship programs," but no training of or criteria for mentors. Identifying mentors who buy into your culture and purpose is absolutely critical.

You might have noticed that many of the strategies outlined here are simply the factors involved in being good human beings who treat each other decently—gratitude, affirmation, connection, social involvement, belonging. All rather obvious, yet overlooked in our organizations. When we integrate them into our everyday culture, they prove invaluable tools in eliciting purpose in the workplace.

PRACTICING PURPOSE TIP

Focus on integrating the three components of meaningful into the key processes of your organization.

An example of how a simple design choice can enhance these tools and transform a workplace comes from Steelcase, an office manufacturing company. In an interview with the magazine *Fast Company*, CEO Jim Keane reflected on his decision to move his long-held leadership team's offices from the top floor of the building down to the first floor, with the account managers and other employees.[7]

PRACTICING PURPOSE TIP

Invest in the whole person. Make sure that what they do makes their whole lives better.

The simple move was meant to increase accessibility, but what followed demonstrates the power of a meaningful workplace. Suddenly, people had access to their leaders. They talked to them daily. Leadership and workers couldn't help interacting. No one could escape social networking, accountability, and an open-door model of feedback.

Highlighting relationships, storytelling, and the impact of the work are critical to building a meaningful organizational culture. Such strategies don't cost a lot of money. They simply mean rethinking how we design organizations to make sure purpose sits at the center of our decisions. The only way to make someone's life better is to know it, so coming into close contact with your people—learning from and about them—is powerful.

PRACTICING PURPOSE EXERCISE

Take a moment and honestly reflect on your team (anyone that works for/with you). For students, focus on the environments you're in. When it comes to fostering meaningful work, what are you currently intentionally doing in each of the dimensions of meaningful work?

How do we make employees / other people feel like they matter and are significant?

How do we connect employees' / other people's work to the greater good or a higher purpose?

How do we help employees' / other people's jobs or work add positive meaning to their lives outside of work?

After answering these questions, where can you improve? What do you do well? What are your reflections?

CHAPTER 10

DESIGNING PURPOSEFUL STAKEHOLDER EXPERIENCES

If you think you're too small to make a difference, try falling asleep with a mosquito in your room.

—*The Dalai Lama*

I was giving a talk to prospective engineers at a prestigious university on using purpose to inspire project teams. At one point in the speech, as I always do, I asked the audience, "Why do you want to be an engineer?"

A man who had been rolling his eyes during the first part of my talk raised his hand. Hoping to stump me, he said, "Well, I guess I'm an engineer because I can't stand people."

The audience gasped, then laughed, but I calmly followed up: "Tell me more. What kind of engineering do you do?"

It turned out he was a biomedical engineer. "So what's at the end of your work in the lab?" I asked.

His answer was "pharmaceutical and biotech companies."

"And what is at the end of what they do?" I asked.

"Buyers," he said. "Sometimes clinics, hospitals."

"And what's at the end of what they do?" I pressed.

"Doctors, nurses," he said. I think he had caught on by this point.

"And they deliver to . . .?"

He sort of grumbled and looked at me and said, "Patients. *People*, I guess."

"Aha," I said, "I guess you *do* love people after all." The audience laughed, and the man smiled, a bit more disarmed.

This simple story represents an important concept: in any industry, in any organization, in anything we undertake, we all are in *human* service. If an organization exists on this planet, there is a human being at the end of its supply or service chain.

IN ANY INDUSTRY, IN ANY ORGANIZATION, IN ANYTHING WE UNDERTAKE, WE ALL ARE IN *HUMAN* SERVICE.

The same is true in our lives and in school. No matter what we do, it inevitably affects people's lives. When we start refocusing on these people, we can start to design experiences that enroll them in our purpose.

The standard for a purposeful organization (or life) rests on this question: *Can every person at every level of your organization, after every personal or digital interaction, know and feel why you exist?*

PRACTICING PURPOSE TIP

Define all possible stakeholders or people who experience your purpose in action.

WHO ARE STAKEHOLDERS?

Stakeholders are human beings. They are all people touched by or involved in what a person or organization does in any way.

Stakeholders can be found in an organization's customer segments, supply channels, investors, revenue streams, critical resources, partnerships, competitors, and daily activities.[1] For individuals, family, friends, coworkers, baristas, mechanics, doctors—anybody one interacts with—can be considered part of a stakeholder world.

One way to identify your stakeholder world is by listing as many stakeholders as possible. For organizations, it's important to list them by name, whenever possible. This necessarily puts their humanness in the foreground. The list becomes what author Paul Ratoff calls your stakeholder world, or your "customers." Taking this reflective exercise further, when you can rank your stakeholders by who experiences or benefits most from your purpose (not products or results), it can dramatically affect how you think about those you impact.

IF AN ORGANIZATION EXISTS ON THIS PLANET, THERE IS A HUMAN BEING AT THE END OF ITS SUPPLY OR SERVICE CHAIN.

For organizations, customers usually rise to the top of the list. But the prevailing assumption of what a customer is can limit the ability to design compelling experiences.

CUSTOMERS ARE HUMANS, TOO

What is a customer? The word was derived from the Latin, *consuetudinarius,* meaning "one to be dealt with." The problem with this definition is that it dehumanizes. If customers are just "ones" to be dealt with, they appear insignificant.

You probably have heard people in your organization or workplace say, "We have to deal with these people," or "We just have to make them happy."

At a recent training session for a group of receptionists, I broke the ice by jokingly asking, "What's the worst part of your job?" One woman raised her hand and said, "When people call."

I laughed at first and then realized she was serious.

Another woman joined in, "Yeah, when we get in at eight in the morning and the phones start ringing off the hook, I just can't stand it." I sort of laughed and asked, "What's your job title again?" They said, "Receptionist."

Their job was literally to receive people, but they had been so conditioned to think of customers as things to avoid, appease, please, or manipulate so that they could get on with their days, they forgot that people were the purpose of their days.

People are our organizations' reason for being, the reason for any job on the planet. But society has conditioned some of us to believe—indeed, the root of the word "customer" itself encourages us to think—they're something to be pushed aside so we can get on with our business. In fact, they *are* our business.

PRACTICING PURPOSE TIP

Redefine customers as human beings; personalize stakeholders.

When I ask people in training sessions what they've learned about customer service, the common answer is that *the customer is always right.* It's no mystery where they learned this mantra. Those of us in customer service (which, if you're breathing oxygen and thinking rationally, is *you*) have made this axiom the bedrock of customer relations.

Legend has it that the phrase itself was born out of the department store and luxury hotel craze of the early 1900s. Hotelier César Ritz, founder of the Ritz-Carlton hotels, supposedly said, "If a diner complains about a dish or the wine, immediately remove it and replace it, no questions asked."

Ritz coined the saying "the customer is always right"—which has gained traction ever since—to deal with customer complaints and make sure the hotel could turn over tables in its dining centers faster—ultimately, to make more money. When we deal with people in this way rather than serving them, they become what we inadvertently define them as—distant obstacles to achieving profit. Perhaps this is why organizations outsource customer service, a $92 billion industry, faster than almost anything else.

This phrase, though, makes little to no sense, and few of those who repeat it ever stop to consider its logic. The problem is simple: it is impossible for a customer to always be right.

Are humans always right?

No.

Then if we say customers "are always right," we're indirectly implying that they're not human.

Many organizations and leaders actively decide to quantify and use those who need their products and services to track profits. The focus becomes measuring the results rather than serving human beings—and the organization's purpose—to inspire those results.

Seeing and serving our customers as the humans they are unleashes the uniquely human ability to create long-lasting connections that foster happiness, fulfillment, and loyalty to our organizations. A renewed focus on *human* service versus *customer* service also allows us to peer into the mirror at the creators of these connections: ourselves.

Charlie Chaplin once said, "We all want to help one another. Human beings are like that. We want to live by each other's happiness, not by each other's misery." Reflecting critically upon the humanity of your organization's customer service delivery plan can be transformative and help convey your purpose. A good place to start is to ask the simple question: *Do we serve people first, and do we serve them well?*

The purposeful design of customer experiences should be simple. Consider your interactions with others in your personal life. How do you know if someone cares about you? What does he or she do or say or look like or sound like to indicate that feeling?

Almost every time I ask these questions in a workshop, participants have answers like these: *he or she looks at you; pays attention to you; asks how you're doing; cares about you; gives you time; listens to you.*

My customer service philosophy is one sentence long: *Go do those things.*

If it were that easy, of course, everyone would have perfect customer service, but designing purposeful experience takes strategy. It requires awakening a compelling purpose, clarifying it, making sure it demonstrates integrity, and finally, delivering it. The daily moment-to-moment interactions at your organization are the most critical for that final piece of the puzzle—delivering purpose. Our smallest actions have the biggest impact.

ELEPHANTS DON'T BITE

In an obscure book from the early 1990s, author Vernon Crawford declared that "elephants don't bite."[2] His point was that while people tend to worry about the big things, small things make the biggest differences. People going on safari in Africa get shots for malaria and other insect-borne illnesses. Once they get there, however, the first elephant or giraffe they encounter consumes their attention. They shoot photos or video of the elephants and send postcards of those giant animals home, while ignoring the potentially deadly little mosquitoes they're slapping off their skin.

This is human nature. We obsess over "big" things and overlook the seemingly small, but the small things matter most. *Elephants don't bite, but mosquitoes do.* It is the small, even tiny things, that have a huge impact

Similarly, organizations focus on the big things—the branding initiative, strategic plan, key meeting, value proposition—while the little things are creating their reputations. How the receptionist out front says hello, how a call is handled, or how an email is returned—these are all-important experiences that when added up become the organization's reputation.

PRACTICING PURPOSE TIP

Optimize the small, everyday experience design at one-on-one levels to inform a larger purpose-delivery strategy.

Consider your own best and worst experiences as a customer—at a supermarket, convenience store, or gas station. The big things were probably similar in all situations. The workers were there on time, wearing name tags, and generally doing their jobs. The "elephants," if you will, were taken care of.

What probably made a difference to you was a worker's tone of voice, a facial expression, attentiveness or inattentiveness, a friendly gesture, or a cold stare. These little things, the mosquitos, define our experiences.

In fact, researchers have found that just 7 percent of what we learn about people comes from their words. Nearly 93 percent of what customers and stakeholders will learn comes from tone of voice, body language, and other nonverbal cues.[3] A digital presence has a kind of body language, too. These little things create billions of experiences every single day.

Reputation, viewed through this lens, becomes quite simple. Does an organization create more positive experiences than negative ones? Reputation is the end sum of the billions of positive and negative experiences created at every level of your organization.

The people who work for an organization are creating these experiences—which suggests that empowering them to know how to fully deliver their *why* through even the smallest of their daily tasks can disproportionately impact reputation and performance.

> REPUTATION IS THE END SUM OF THE BILLIONS OF POSITIVE AND NEGATIVE EXPERIENCES CREATED AT EVERY LEVEL OF YOUR ORGANIZATION.

In fact, these little experiences are so powerful, it is almost impossible to redeem a single negative experience. Researchers have found that it takes up to three positive experiences to overcome a negative one.[4] The stakes then are incredibly high when people interact with a product or service and come away with some sense of why a person or organization exists.

Consider these well-documented facts regarding customer service:[5]

- Customers will spend up to 10 percent more for the same product if it's offered with better service.

- When people receive good service, they tell ten to twelve people on average.

- When people receive poor service, they tell twenty-five to forty people on average.

- There is an 82 percent chance that customers will repurchase from a company where they were satisfied.

- There is a 91 percent chance that a poor experience will dissuade a customer from ever going back to a company.

The stakes are high not only because organizations and people want to deliver a good service or experience. Each interaction is also about compelling people to join a cause and help deliver purpose. As we've explored, purpose taps into people's psychological desire to make the world better and do good. Purpose permeates every behavior and thought in an organization. It's a reason worth committing to that inspires service to the greater good.

This holds true with customers too. Customers and investors—and all the stakeholders listed earlier in this chapter—are people who want to do good, get involved in our cause, and know our purpose through the experiences we design for them.

THE LIPTON TEA STORY

One strategy for engaging customers on this deeper level involves considering how the people served feel part of a movement after they've bought something from or committed to an organization. After all, people buy from "companies," they follow "leaders," but they JOIN movements. How are they kept involved in the organization's purpose?

Human beings rely on stories to make sense of the world, and customers are no exception. Telling the story of how a company helps to deliver their purpose can encourage stakeholders to commit emotionally to an organization or brand.

> AFTER ALL, PEOPLE BUY FROM "COMPANIES," THEY FOLLOW "LEADERS," BUT THEY JOIN MOVEMENTS.

Here are a few tips to start the process:

- Show people where products are made and who makes them. Put the faces of employees out there for people to see. Let them hear the story.

- Take customers and stakeholders on a journey of purpose to see the origins of materials.

- Have customers themselves tell stories about how a product or service is changing the world and helping their lives.

- Consistently strategize: which services or products can make the world a better place and how is this a business opportunity?

A popular tea company offers a powerful example of an organization engaging stakeholders in its purpose. Lipton tea consciously strategized about what the company wanted its consumers thinking as they drank their morning beverage.

Lipton put a picture of a real tea farmer working one of the sustainable plantations that supply the company on each box of tea. Next to the photo appeared a story connecting these farmers to Lipton's partnership with the Rainforest Alliance, one of the most impactful NGOs working on the rainforests. The Alliance provides people with meaningful work in sustainable ways, which in turn is helping to save our rainforests. Simply opening a package of tea now connects Lipton customers with the company's *why* and a compelling, world-changing purpose.[6]

PRACTICING PURPOSE TIP

Assess how you involve all of your stakeholders in your purpose that is detached from results.

Lipton thought about its customers as humans, sitting down in the morning and steeping their tea.

What should stakeholders think about and feel beyond simply having a product or service? How are they emotionally invited into delivering a purpose? How are experiences engineered, right down to tone of voice and the nonverbal expressions of employees?

The answer to these questions can be the ultimate competitive advantage in delivering purpose.

 # PRACTICING PURPOSE EXERCISE

Delivering Purpose Action Plan

Complete the following statements. Be as specific as possible and repeat for each stakeholder group identified.

4. We/I exist in the world to . . .

5. [INSERT STAKEHOLDER GROUP] will be able to tell by . . .

6. In every physical or digital interaction with [INSERT STAKE-HOLDER GROUP], we will:

    say . . .

    sound (tone) . . .

    appear . . .

    do . . .

CHAPTER 11

HOW TO START

*Efforts and courage are not enough
without purpose and direction.*

—*John F. Kennedy*

While the transformational power of the invisible leader, authentic purpose, is clear, implementing it in our lives, leadership, and organizations can be daunting. Frequently, people are not sure where to begin.

It is important to note in this final chapter that purpose is a process. It is ongoing, not a one-time exercise or achievement. It requires deep reflection and a willingness to deviate from mainstream notions regarding how to motivate ourselves and others, and how to design organizations.

My own vision for organizations and society is largely aspirational. I imagine a future in which all people are on fire about their lives and work. They're passionate and other-focused, and they have a clear, compelling reason for existence that inspires them and the people in their organizations to get out of bed every single day.

Purpose is not an event. It's not a book. It's not an overnight change. It's not one statement. It is an intentional process that takes clear visioning and a clear plan. So how do you start?

I've identified four major elements that correspond to meaningful change in living and leading with purpose:

1. Thinking in abundance

2. Setting a clear vision, rooted in purpose

3. Identifying barriers

4. Reassessing purpose

THINKING IN ABUNDANCE

In addition to setting a purposeful mindset of believing work matters, benefitting others, and proving purpose consistently, it is important to start thinking in abundance.

Many leaders, and most of us, lead our organizations and lives from a scarcity mindset—constantly thinking there's not enough money, change is dangerous, risk is bad, and failure is a limitation.

People tend to make many decisions based on such delusions of scarcity.

Scarcity thinking is one of the things that I've noticed has led us into the purpose drought. When I started my own speaking and consulting business, this was how I initially thought too. *I'm too young. I haven't written a book. I'm too inexperienced. There aren't any clients. There isn't any money to be made out there. The market is too competitive. People won't want to buy into this purpose stuff.*

PRACTICING PURPOSE TIP

Shift from a scarcity mindset to an abundance mindset. Every person and organization can be purposeful.

My performance and behaviors reflected this negative mindset. I would spend days lamenting my bad luck and the choice to quit my job and pursue a speaking and consulting career. I secretly almost applied for salaried jobs again just to have the illusion of security. A scarcity mindset led me, the person writing the book about purpose, into a lack of purpose.

Then, in an instant, I changed my outlook. I started thinking, *There are thousands of potential clients out there. There is an abundance of money to be made. I can write a book. I can make a living doing this. People need purpose. People want purpose.* I started researching and finding a way to deliver my purpose. One of the ways I'm accomplishing it is through writing the book you're reading today. My new awareness of the abundance of opportunities out there motivated me to go and get them.

The same change in attitude can work for people in organizations trying to make the shift to being purposeful. I think we need to start asking, what can we do? How can we find a way to become purposeful and awaken the invisible leader today? Who can we be?

Scarcity thinking prompts reaction. Abundance thinking prompts action. And action is the way forward.

Before we start delivering purpose, adopting an abundance mindset is critical.

> **SCARCITY THINKING PROMPTS REACTION. ABUNDANCE THINKING PROMPTS ACTION. AND ACTION IS THE WAY FORWARD.**

SETTING A CLEAR VISION ROOTED IN PURPOSE

In conjunction with focusing on abundance, it's critical to set a clear vision of what our organizations and our lives would look and feel like if we were living purposefully. It's tough to enact a plan to get there without a vision of the destination.

To do this, embracing creative tension is critical. Creative tension is the gap between who we are and who we want to be.[1] And it is in this space that creativity, imagination, and innovation thrive. Take the time to step back and ask, what do we want as an organization? What do I want in my life? Why do we want it? How can we actually get there from a purpose-oriented perspective? Answering these questions is incredibly powerful.

Unfortunately, in my work with organizations and individuals, I've noted that visioning often stops after brainstorming what we want—or it's disguised in organizations as a strategic plan. This result is generally more of a wish list than a true vision. Vague hopes are a good start only if we go deeper to design a vision that prompts decisive action and purposeful behavior. A wish becomes a vision the moment it has a plan.

> **A WISH BECOMES A VISION THE MOMENT IT HAS A PLAN.**

HOW TO SET A CLEAR VISION

Having a framework to begin setting a vision is helpful. And through my work with individuals and teams working toward purposeful visions for their organizations, I found that an actionable vision aligns three critical facets of our organizational and personal lives: feeling, being, and doing.

PRACTICING PURPOSE TIP

Set a clear, purpose-aligned vision of the desired state of your organization/life.

Set aside an ample amount of uninterrupted time for you or your leadership team to begin "visioning." If you're doing this with an organization, have people shut off their phones and their computers, and make sure they take a social media fast of at least twenty-four hours so they're focused on the organization. Visioning is too important to squeeze into a few impulsive moments at the end of a meeting, a two-hour retreat, or a working lunch. Start by asking the following three critical questions of yourself and your organization.

As you set out to answer these questions, begin with this statement: *If we were a purposeful organization . . .* Or you can phrase it, *If I were leading with purpose . . .*

1. **How would it feel?** If your organization or life was in its ideal state from a purpose-oriented perspective a year from now, how would you feel? For organizations, how would it feel to work there? Be as specific and imaginative as possible, and focus on emotion. For example, you might say, people who work for us would *feel* content or enthusiastic.

   Imagine yourself in that purposeful organization or life a year from now. How would it feel to talk about your work and your life? How would it feel to be at your job on a daily basis? By identifying how we want to feel in organizations, we tap into the emotional component we've been exploring in this book—the one so critical in our efforts to engage people.

2. **Who do I/we have to *be* to feel that way?** What qualities would you have to exhibit to feel each of the emotions you wrote down? Instead of focusing on feelings here, complete this statement: *I need to be . . .* I recommend brainstorming a "being" quality for each feeling you wrote down. For example, if you said, I want people to *feel* enthusiastic, they might need to *be* committed. To *feel* content, you might need to *be* mindful.

This process is also helpful in identifying the values explored in the chapter on the integrity of purpose. The being qualities that produce the feelings outlined in your vision generally correspond to your values. Focus people's minds on personal development and away from to-do lists and results. I always say that "to be" lists are far more powerful than "to do" lists.

3. **What do I have to *do*?** Activation is the final and most important step in clear visioning. Ask, what are the activities, people, places, and things that will help you *be* who you need to be and *feel* what you want to feel?

    Ask, what specific actions will we take? When do we need to take these actions? Align each action with a "being" and "feeling" quality you previously noted. Be specific. For instance, you might say, "I want people to *feel* content, so we need to *be* mindful. Teaching our people techniques to manage stress will help get us there." This is a vision plan. The actions that align to your ideal *being* and *feeling* qualities become your plan moving forward.

Your actions as an organization or a leader are firmly rooted in your vision, which is firmly rooted in your purpose. Taking this decisive action is the first step toward becoming more purposeful.

IDENTIFYING AND REMOVING BARRIERS

After we set a clear vision, it's important to identify and remove barriers to living and leading with purpose. The following is a powerful exercise for both teams and individuals, derived from Kurt Lewin's *Force Field Analysis* work:[2]

1. We have our vision. Now ask, why is it a vision and not the current reality? Describe the current realities of your organization and life in the same level of detail you used to craft your vision. What are the common behaviors? How do people currently feel in your organization? What are the current values? This process can be eye-opening and a key element in the creative tension between who you are and who you want to be.

PRACTICING PURPOSE TIP

Identify catalysts to being purposeful and identify barriers. Focus resources on mitigating barriers and reinforcing catalysis.

---

2. Identify the catalysts. What do you do well? When you are operating purposefully, what specifically are you doing? One of my favorite questions to have people ask themselves is: *What do we do when we do what we do well?* What things happen in the organization when we are delivering our purpose? Write the specifics down. They are the catalysts

you will want to invest resources in. You will want to

WHAT DO WE DO WHEN WE DO WHAT WE DO WELL?

surround yourself with people who help you to do those things.

3. Identify the barriers. Ask, what keeps us from being purposeful, from awakening and clarifying purpose? What gets in the way of our integrity and consistency? Be specific. Time, stress, capacity—these are fine starting points, but detail the various roadblocks. What are the worst constraints on time? Label particular bottlenecks or stressors. This is where I emphasize that purpose is not easy. The barriers can be significant.

4. Focus your resources on mitigating the barriers you have identified. Eliminating or shrinking barriers becomes your organizational development plan, one that's purpose-centered and rooted in your vision. At the same time, it's critical to invest in maintaining the catalysts so you have the power to move into the desired state.

CREATE SPECIFIC GOALS AND OBJECTIVES

Once you do this exercise, build specific goals and objectives into your strategic plan. Many readers probably have heard of SMART goals. The acronym can vary, but the letters generally stand for goals that are Specific, Measurable, Achievable, Relevant, and Time-bound. I would add that they should also be rooted in purpose—but, in any case, the idea is to make your objectives concrete.

For example, if you're a nonprofit whose purpose is to end homelessness, your goal might be to make sure that fifteen people find homes within six months. As an organization, you agree that making fifteen contacts per week is an effective way to achieve this goal.

Whatever field you're in, you can find templates that will help you set effective goals, but making sure they are concrete and *aligned with your purpose* is the key to achieving the vision you created.

ASSESSMENT

Finally, I encourage you to do an initial assessment regarding purpose and then follow it with regular, ongoing assessments. As I've emphasized, purpose is a process, not a one-time exercise, and maintaining it requires constant reflection. A full, detailed assessment and other tools can be found on my website, www.zachmercurio.com/tools. I have broken this assessment into the major areas we've covered in this book: purpose awakening, purpose clarity, purpose consistency and integrity, and purpose delivery.

Any organization, from a Fortune 500 company to a nonprofit to a family can use this assessment and these questions. The science of purpose is interdisciplinary, and the principles apply broadly.

PURPOSE AWAKENING

- Do we have a collective belief that the work matters at all levels of our lives and organizations? If not, where is this lacking?

- Do we have a clear understanding of the human problem we exist to solve?

- Is solving that human problem at the forefront of our everyday practices?

- Do we regularly interface with the people impacted by our lives, products, and services?

- Are the people we employ or who are involved in our movements shown why the work matters before they are shown what to do?

PURPOSE CLARITY

- Is there a clear, common reason for existence in our life and organization, one that is truly believed?

- Is that reason for existence clearly stated, compelling, and other-focused?

- Does our purpose statement include the components of an effective purpose statement?

- Is that purpose statement detached from results?

- Is the purpose clear to the organization and understood in common language?

- Is the purpose visible on a daily basis?

- Do we know our purpose statement and believe it?

- Does the environment we have designed reinforce the clearly stated purpose?

PURPOSE CONSISTENCY AND INTEGRITY

- Are the values of our lives or organizations clearly aligned with our authentic purpose?

- Do we have a decision-making process that is purpose-centered?

- Is it shared by people we work with?

- Are our goals connected to our purpose or focused on our results?

- Do we create space between external pressure and our decision making regularly?

PURPOSE DELIVERY

- Do we have an experience-design plan that specifically articulates how stakeholders will know and feel our purpose?

- Have we intentionally designed environments, practices, policies, and procedures around our purpose?

- Do our stakeholder-assessment and evaluation tools measure how people we interact with feel about our purpose? Do they measure emotional commitment?

- Does our marketing and branding tell the story of *why* we do what we do or simply tell the story of *what* we do?

- Do our value propositions start with our *why*?

As you start asking these questions, you'll uncover areas of your organization and life where purpose isn't aligned. It's important to maintain that abundance mindset and not retreat into behaviors and strategies that might have allowed us to drift in the past. Keep revisiting the vision you created.

Because this is a process, I would encourage you to continually refer back to this book. As you go through the assessment, reread chapters focused on areas where you need reinforcement. Ask yourself these assessment questions every day, as I do. I could not have written this book without my own constant, critical self-reflection on purpose alignment.

I also encourage you to create a community of purpose. Surround yourself with people in your area, with organizational leaders, friends, and family members who believe in purpose. Create a purposeful leader community. Often, we like to keep these things private, but purpose by its nature involves others.

As we explored at the beginning of this book, the search for meaning and purpose is fundamentally human, and human beings thrive on community. As you develop and deliver your authentic purpose, community offers support, encouragement, and ideas—plus it makes us accountable. Peer accountability is key to delivering your *why*.

PRACTICING PURPOSE TIP

Do an initial purpose assessment and continually reassess the major areas outlined in this book.

I hope that by this point you feel closer to your unique and authentic world-changing reason for existence. Once we awaken that reason for existing and bring people into our movements—both as individuals and organizations—the possibilities of our impact on this world are limitless.

 PRACTICING PURPOSE EXERCISE

Develop a clear purpose-oriented vision using the guidelines in this chapter.

THE CONTINUAL SEARCH FOR PURPOSE

The idea of awakening, clarifying, and delivering purpose can seem daunting. I have written at times about shifting the paradigms that underlie our institutions and society, but it wasn't my goal to make purpose appear intimidating or unattainable—just the opposite.

I want to leave you with a quote from the German philosopher Johann Fichte. In *The Vocation of Man,* he wrote, "You could not remove a single grain of sand from its place without thereby changing something throughout all parts of the immeasurable whole."

If we set out to change society, we're likely to freeze up or feel paralyzed, but if we set out to find the small places in our organizations and in our lives that we can change, we end up having a big, immeasurable impact. Shift that grain of sand, as Fichte said, and you will change parts throughout the immeasurable whole.

If you were at all moved by this book to create a life and/or organization with purpose, the shifts you begin to make can be small. Even minute tweaks of perspective, day in and day out, can have a far-reaching impact. Simply realizing what the invisible leader is, becoming aware of the power of authentic purpose, has an immediate effect and can lead to deep change.

I am an optimist when it comes to people and organizations. I imagine a society, an economy, and a world in which every person and every leader in an organization is inspired by and built on purpose. I want to compel people to imagine that world as well, and to commit to being a part of its design.

Purpose, however, as I have written repeatedly in these pages, is a process. It doesn't arrive overnight, and it isn't easy. Doing the small things that dramatically change your mindset over time requires regularly circling back to make sure your purpose is aligned and present throughout your life and organization.

Revisit the exercises at the end of each chapter periodically, and retake the assessment that concluded chapter 11. This will not only highlight places where you might be falling short or need greater effort; it will also mark your progress and demonstrate how far you've traveled down the path to greater purpose.

I hope that you will share this book and this message with those around you, too. Surrounding yourself with purposeful people, as I've pointed out, is one of the biggest steps to developing a purposeful mindset and realizing the transforming power of the invisible leader.

THE PATH TO PURPOSE

PURPOSE
DELIVERY

PURPOSE
CONSISTENCY

PURPOSE
CLARITY

PURPOSE
AWAKENING

SOURCES

CHAPTER 1 SOURCES

1. Simon Sinek, "How great leaders inspire action," TEDxPuget Sound, September 2009.

2. Aaron Hurst, *Purpose Economy* (Elevate, 2014).

3. Viktor E. Frankl, *Man's Search for Meaning* (Simon and Schuster, 1985).

4. Greg Ayers, "Martin Luther's View of Faith and Work" *Institute for Faith, Work & Economics*, October 31, 2012, https://tifwe.org/martin-luthers-view-of-faith-work/.

5. Martin Luther, *On the Babylonian Captivity of the Church*, October 1520.

6. Roger B. Hill, "History of Work Ethic" University of Georgia, last updated August 10, 2012, http://workethic.coe.uga.edu/hatcp.html.

7. Steve Taylor, "The Power of Purpose," *Psychology Today*, July 21, 2013, https://www.psychologytoday.com/blog/out-the-darkness/201307/the-power-purpose.

CHAPTER 2 SOURCES

1. Ali Binazir, "What are the chances of your coming into being?" June 15, 2011, http://blogs.harvard.edu/abinazir/2011/06/15/what-are-chances-you-would-be-born/.

2. Fritz Heider and Marianne Simmel, "An experimental study of apparent behavior," *The American Journal of Psychology* 57, no. 2 (1944): 243–259.

3. Nancy C. Morse and Rober S. Weiss, "The function and meaning of work and the job," *American Sociological Review* 20, no. 2 (1955): 191–198.

4. Viktor E. Frankl, *Man's Search for Meaning* (Simon and Schuster, 1985).

5. Reginald W. Bibby, *Canada's Teens: Today, Yesterday, and Tomorrow* (Toronto: Stoddart, 2001).

6. R. Cohen, C. Bavishi, and A. Rozanski, "Purpose in life and its relationship to all-cause mortality and cardiovascular events: A meta-analysis," *Psychosomatic medicine* 78, no. 2 (2016): 122–133.

7. Patti Neighmond, "People Who Feel They Have A Purpose In Life Live Longer," NPR, July 28, 2014, http://www.npr.org/sections/health-shots/2014/07/28/334447274/people-who-feel-they-have-a-purpose-in-life-live-longer.

8. Gallup, "State of Global Well-Being," 2014, http://info.healthways.com/hubfs/Well-Being_Index/2014_Data/Gallup-Healthways_State_of_Global_Well-Being_2014_Country_Rankings.pdf.

9. Richard J. Leider, *The Power of Purpose: Creating Meaning in Your Life and Work* (Berrett-Koehler Publishers, 2015).

10. LinkedIn, "Purpose at Work: 2016 Global Report," 2016, https://business.linkedin.com/talent-solutions/job-trends/purpose-at-work.

11. Devin Thorpe, "New Report: 'Purpose-Oriented' Employees 'Outperform,'" *Forbes*, December 22, 2015, http://www.forbes.com/sites/devinthorpe/2015/12/22/4988/#401ebda67d7b.

12. Michael F. Steger, Bryan J. Dik, and Ryan D. Duffy, "Measuring meaningful work: The work and meaning inventory (WAMI)," *Journal of Career Assessment* (2012): 322–337.

13. Bryan J. Dik and Ryan D. Duffy, *Make Your Job a Calling: How the Psychology of Vocation Can Change Your Life at Work* (Templeton Foundation Press, 2012).

14. Jim C. Collins and Jerry I. Porras, *Built to Last: Successful Habits of Visionary Companies* (Random House, 2005).

15. Jim Stengel, *Grow: How Ideals Power Growth and Profit at the World's 50 Greatest Companies* (Random House, 2012).

16. Ernst & Young Beacon Institute, "The Business Case for Purpose," *Harvard Business Review*, 2005, http://www.ey.com/Publication/vwLUAssets/ey-the-business-case-for-purpose/$FILE/ey-the-business-case-for-purpose.pdf.

17. D. S. Yeager et al., "Boring but important: A self-transcendent purpose for learning fosters academic self-regulation," *Journal of Personality and Social Psychology* 107, no. 4 (2014): 559.

CHAPTER 3 SOURCES

1. "The Gospel According to Mac," *30 for 30,* ESPN, directed by Jim Podhoretz.

2. Kyle Ringo, "1990 national championship flashback: Bill McCartney, maestro of motivation," *Daily Camera*, August 20, 2015, http://www.dailycamera.com/ci_28673015/1990-national-championship-flashback-bill-mccartney-maestro-motivation.

3. Nanette Monin and Ralph Bathurst, "Mary Follett on the leadership of 'Everyman,'" *ephemera* 8 no. 4 (2008): 447–46.

4. Gill Robinson Hickman, *Leading Organizations: Perspectives for a New Era* (Sage Publications, 1998).

5. Peter Guy Northouse, *Leadership: Theory and Practice* (Sage Publications, 2015).

6. Kendra Cherry, "The Major Leadership Theories: The Eight Major Theories of Leadership," October 5, 2016, https://www.verywell.com/leadership-theories-2795323.

CHAPTER 4 SOURCES

1. Amanda Onion, "Science Behind the Butterfly Effect," ABC News, January 23, 2017, http://abcnews.go.com/Technology/story?id=99596&page=1.

2. "Putting a Face to a Name: The Art of Motivating Employees," Wharton: University of Pennsylvania, February 17, 2010, http://knowledge.wharton.upenn.edu/article/putting-a-face-to-a-name-the-art-of-motivating-employees/.

3. Adam M. Grant at al., "Impact and the art of motivation maintenance: The effects of contact with beneficiaries on persistence behavior," *Organizational Behavior and Human Decision Processes* 103, no. 1 (2007): 53–67.

4. Bruce N. Pfau, "How An Accounting Firm Convinced Its Employees They Could Change The World," *Harvard Business Review*, October 6, 2015, https://hbr.org/2015/10/how-an-accounting-firm-convinced-its-employees-they-could-change-the-world.

5. Lisa Earle McLeod, *Selling with Noble Purpose: How to Drive Revenue and Do Work That Makes You Proud* (John Wiley & Sons, 2012).

6. R. Q. Quiroga et al., "Invariant visual representation by single neurons in the human brain," *Nature* 435, no. 7045 (2005): 1102–1107.

7. Ron Gutman, "The Hidden Power of Smiling," TED Talk, 2011.

CHAPTER 5 SOURCES

1. Katya Andreson, "What motivates donors? Two new studies say," Network for Good, November 14, 2012, http://www.networkforgood.com/nonprofitblog/what-motivates-donors-two-new-studies-say/.

2. Gone Adventurin, http://www.goneadventurin.com/.

3. Blake Mycoskie, *Start Something That Matters* (Spiegel & Grau, 2012).

4. Brene Brown, "The Power of Vulnerability," TED Talk, 2010, http://www.ted.com/talks/brene_brown_on_vulnerability.

5. Charles Poladian, "The Surprising Health Benefits of Empathy," Medical Daily, 2012, http://www.medicaldaily.com/surprising-health-effects-empathy-240983.

6. Heather Marie Higgins, "Empathy training and stress: Their role in medical students' responses to emotional patients," University of British Columbia, doctoral dissertation, 2011.

7. Edward P. Weber and Anne M. Khademian, "Wicked problems, knowledge challenges, and collaborative capacity builders in network settings," *Public Administration Review* (2008).

8. UN Sustainable Development Goals, http://www.un.org/sustainabledevelopment/sustainable-development-goals/.

CHAPTER 6 SOURCES

1. George Serafeim and Claudine Gartenberg, "The Type of Purpose That Makes Companies More Profitable." *Harvard Business Review*, October 21, 2016, https://hbr.org/2016/10/the-type-of-purpose-that-makes-companies-more-profitable.

2. William Deresiewicz, *Excellent Sheep: The Miseducation of the American Elite and the Way to a Meaningful Life* (Simon and Schuster, 2014).

3. Gail Matthews, "Goals research summary," Dominican University (2013).

4. Peter M. Senge, "The fifth discipline," *Measuring Business Excellence* 1, no. 3 (1997): 46–51.

5. Simon Sinek, *Start with Why: How Great Leaders Inspire Everyone to Take Action* (Penguin, 2009).

6. Jeff James, "Common Purpose: How to Inspire Your Staff," Disney Institute, September 25, 2012, https://disneyinstitute.com/blog/2012/09/common-purpose-how-to-inspire-your-staff/100/.

CHAPTER 7 SOURCES

1. Erik Vance, "Unlocking the Healing Power of You," *National Geographic*, 2016, http://www.nationalgeographic.com/magazine/2016/12/healing-science-belief-placebo/.

2. Ananya Mandal, "Dopamine Functions," News Medical, last updated October 27, 2015, http://www.news-medical.net/health/Dopamine-Functions.aspx.

3. Alex Lickerman, "The Two Kinds of Belief," *Psychology Today*, April 24, 2011, https://www.psychologytoday.com/blog/happiness-in-world/201104/the-two-kinds-belief.

4. Roy Spence and Haley Rushing, *It's Not What You Sell, It's What You Stand For*, (Brilliance Audio, 2008).

5. "Eco-friendly product claims often misleading," NPR, November 30, 2007, http://www.npr.org/templates/story/story.php?storyId=16754919.

6. Jenny Anderson, "This is what work-life balance looks like at a company with 100% retention of moms," Quartz, October 16, 2016, https://qz.com/806516/the-secret-to-patagonias-success-keeping-moms-and-onsite-child-care-and-paid-parental-leave/.

CHAPTER 8 SOURCES

1. Wells Fargo, "Vision and Mission," https://www.wellsfargomedia.com/pdf/invest_relations/VisionandValues04.pdf.

2. Wells Fargo, "Culture of Caring," https://www.wellsfargo.com/about/corporate/vision-and-values/our-culture/.

3. Lisa D. Ordóñez, Maurice E. Schweitzer, Adam D. Galinsky, and Max H. Bazerman, "Goals gone wild: The systematic side effects of overprescribing goal setting," *Harvard Business School* 23, no. 1 (2009): 6–16.

4. Robert B. Cialdini, Raymond R. Reno, and Carl A. Kallgren, "A focus theory of normative conduct: Recycling the concept of norms to reduce littering in public places," *Journal of Personality and Social Psychology* 58, no. 6 (1990): 1015–1026.

5. Robert J. Nash, *"Real World" Ethics: Frameworks for Educators and Human Service Professionals* (Teachers College Press, 2002).

CHAPTER 9 SOURCES

1. Studs Terkel, *Working: People Talk about What They Do All Day and How They Feel about What They Do* (The New Press, 1974).

2. Michael F. Steger, Bryan J. Dik, and Ryan D. Duffy, "Measuring meaningful work: The work and meaning inventory (WAMI)," *Journal of Career Assessment* (2012): 322–337.

3. Nancy K. Schlossberg, "Marginality and mattering: Key issues in building community," *New Directions for Student Services* 48 (1989): 5–15.

4. Sloane R. Weitzel, (2008). *Feedback That Works: How to Build and Deliver Your Message* (Chicago: Center for Creative leadership, 2000).

5. Elizabeth Wolfe Morrison, "Newcomers' Relationships: The Role of Social Network Ties during Socialization," *Academy of Management Journal* 45, no. 6 (2002): 1149–1160.

6. Zach A. Mercurio, "Affective commitment as a core essence of organizational commitment: an integrative literature review," *Human Resource Development Review* 14, no. 4 (2015): 389–414.

7. Aaron Hurst, "How Steelcase Rearranged Its Workplace to Create a Purposeful Office, *Fast Company,* December 8, 2016, https://www.fastcoexist.com/3066391/the-purposeful-ceo/how-steelcase-rearranged-its-workplace-to-create-a-purposeful-office.

CHAPTER 10 SOURCES

1. Paul Ratoff, *Thriving in a Stakeholder World: Purpose as the New Competitive Advantage* (Indie Books International, 2015).

2. Vernon Crawford, *Elephants Don't Bite: How Doing the Little Things Right Can Make a Big Difference in Your Career and Your Life* (Good Thyme Books, 1991).

3. Albert Mehrabian, *Nonverbal Communication* (Transaction Publishers, 1972).

4. Michele M. Tugade and Barbara L. Fredrickson, "Resilient individuals use positive emotions to bounce back from negative emotional experiences," *Journal of Personality and Social Psychology* 86, no. 2 (2004): 320.

5. "Customer Service Facts," *CSM,* http://www.customerservicemanager.com/customer-service-facts/.

6. Zach Mercurio, "Why It Pays to Find Your Company's Global Purpose," Huffington Post, December 22, 2016, http://www.huffingtonpost.com/zach-mercurio it-pays-to-find-your-comp_b_13586988.html.

CHAPTER 11 SOURCES

1. Peter M. Senge, *The Fifth Discipline: The Art and Practice of the Learning Organization* (Doubleday, 2006).

2. Kurt Lewin, "Force Field Analysis," *The 1973 Annual Handbook for Group Facilitators,* 111–13.